How to Survive

TURNING 5

REGINA SKYER, ESQ.

CONTENTS

How to Survive Turning 5: A Guide for NYC Parents of Special Needs Children

Copyright © 2015 by Regina Skyer, Esq.
Illustrations copyright © 2015 by Wendy Borges
Production and layout by Nicheworks Technology & Design

Includes contents. 1. Introduction 2. An Overview 3. Getting Started 4. Special Education Private Schools
5. Pendency 6. Due Process Impartial Hearing 7. Private Evaluations 8. Learning the Language

ISBN: 978-0-692-53834-0 Paperback

Printed in the United States of America

"We are here to do good. It is the responsibility of every human being to aspire to do something worthwhile, to make this world a better place than the one he found. Life is a gift, and if we agree to accept it, we must contribute in return."

Albert Einstein

INTRODUCTION

If you are reading this book, you are most likely part of a growing legion of parents and caregivers who have a young child with special needs. Regardless of the label or diagnosis that your child has, what you all have in common is a special type of worry and concern. It's this worry that wakes up with you in the morning and goes to bed with you at night. However, it's this worry that has also turned you into the best and most tenacious protector and advocate for your child.

This book is based on my work with children with special needs and their parents for over 40 years. It will serve as your guide and sourcebook for navigating the CSE turning-five process in New York City, hopefully bringing you comfort as well as knowledge.

New York City—The Capital of Special Education

The New York City Department of Education, commonly referred to as the DOE, is the largest school district in the United States. New York City public schools have responsibility for over 1.4 million students every year, with approximately fifteen percent of them identified as having special needs and requiring some kind of special education or related services. For the school year 2014-2015, the DOE's total budget was $25.9 billion dollars. This is larger than the gross national product of Uruguay or Lebanon! It is therefore not surprising that parents feel like they are entering a foreign country when they deal with the DOE.

In June 2002, Mayor Michael Bloomberg took control of education away from what was known as the Board of Education (BOE) and established a new City agency known as the Department of Education (DOE). Although the board still exists, technically, as the governing body of the DOE, its members are now appointed by the Mayor and the five borough presidents and have far less control and influence than they had prior to 2002.

On paper, there is only one school district for all of New York City. However, due to the magnitude of students, the DOE has subdivided itself into 10 Regions and 32 Districts. The region or district that is responsible for any given child is determined either by where the family resides or where the child attends school. Each region has its own Committee on Special Education (CSE).

The question of who has "jurisdiction" or responsibility for developing an Individualized Education Program (IEP) for a child can be confusing, and I will talk more about this later on in the book. For all children who are turning five years of age, their initial "Turning Five Review Meeting" must occur in the district or region where the child resides.

TIP
For a directory of CSE offices based on a child's home address, see
the chart "CSE Regions and Districts" at the end of Chapter One.

The DOE is one of the most complex, bureaucratic agencies that New York City has. It is a world unto itself, with its own language, regulations, and rules. Simply learning the language is enough to frighten a parent who is entering the system at a time when they are most vulnerable. Since learning and understanding the new DOE language is critical in accessing programs and services, I have created a Comprehensive Glossary at the end of this book. If there is a term or word that I have not included, please email me for the answer.

I often refer to New York City as "the capital of special education." It is Nirvana for those who understand the processes and know how to access the system. Our city is home to the best special education schools and programs in the world, including some innovative public schools. I am awestruck by the wealth of opportunity within our own five boroughs, yet amazed at the lack of a directory to guide parents through the process and to help them find the right programs, professionals, and schools for their child. It is simple to get 50 recommendations for a hairdresser, but just try to find a child psychiatrist who responds to phone calls, or a neuropsychologist who is familiar with and can help find the right special needs school. Unfortunately, there is no guide that talks about the different categories of private schools, or how to maximize a child's chance of getting into such a school, or how to obtain funding or reimbursement for the tuition costs. Throughout this book I will be providing you with tips to address these concerns.

TIP
There is a well-defined parent underground and several internet
parent chat rooms that are valuable sources of information.
Parents should become familiar with these sites. Keep in mind that
the advice given is highly subjective. These sites are a good starting
point, but never a substitute for your own judgment about your child.

How To Survive...

My original intention was to write a single book that would cover infancy through young adulthood. I realized very early on in my research and writing that there was far too much information for me to consolidate into one book. Instead, along with my amazing staff, I am working on a series of books that will do this.

The first in the series, *How to Survive the Early Years of a Special Needs Child*, will address the needs and concerns of parents who have discovered that their child has disabilities or special needs very early in their life. Readers will learn all about the federal program known as "Early Intervention," which is free and available to all parents who have children with, or are suspected of having, developmental delays. This book will also help parents as their children exit Early Intervention and transition into the Committee on Preschool Special Education (CPSE).

The second book in the series, *How to Survive Turning 5,* is the book you are now reading. This book will guide parents through the entry process into the school-age unit of the Committee on Special Education (CSE).

The third book in the series, *How to Survive Special Education in New York City—The Real Special Education Handbook*, will be designed specifically for parents of school-aged children (ages 5 through 21). This book will guide parents through all available private and public school options and also explain the transition out of the Department of Education.

The fourth book in the series, *How to Survive After High School*, will help parents as their teenager or young adult ages out of and leaves the public school system.

The fifth book in the series, *How to Survive a Residential School Placement* will help parents understand and tackle a painful decision—having to place their child in a residential school.

I have started this series, out of order; *How to Survive Turning 5* is the first publication because of the vast number of parents seeking my advice at the critical juncture when their children are transitioning out of CPSE, about to enter the CSE. The need to reach these parents as soon as possible is what motivated me to first write about the turning-five process.

Many parents come to my firm for a consultation in order to understand their options and the process. However, not all parents have the resources to do this. It is important to me to get the information that I have accumulated in over forty years of work in the special education community out to as many parents as possible.

The highly regarded agency, **Advocates for Children**, distributes a publication entitled: *Turning 5: A Guide to the Transition from Preschool Special Education to Kindergarten* (www.advocatesforchildren.org/sites/default/files/library/turning_5_guide.pdf). Similarly, the DOE annually publishes *Kindergarten: An Orientation Guide for Families of Students with Disabilities* (www.advocatesforchildren.org/sites/default/files/library/turning_5_guide.pdf). These are helpful publications that provide parents with a technical overview of the entry process into New York City public schools.

How to Survive Turning 5 and my subsequent books will go a step further than these free publications. They will include my own insights and general advice as well as detailed case studies based on actual clients I have represented. You will also find charts throughout this book. In 1988, when I went to law school, the only way I was able to synthesize and process the huge amount of information that I was learning was to create charts and diagrams. I have continued doing this throughout my legal career, and hope you find this way of organizing as helpful as I do.

I have and will continue to address current issues that relate to special education in NYC in my blog at *www.skyerlaw.com*. There has been a great deal of talk and excitement, for example, about the policy memorandum that Mayor de Blasio issued in June 2014, which includes changes to settlement practice. We are all hopeful that this is the first step in making special education programs more accessible.

It might help to think of special education services and programs as a highway with on and off exits. Nobody wants to be on this road, but since you are, I promise you that you will meet wonderful people and have meaningful experiences along the way. Throughout this book you will hear my voice. It is a voice filled with hope, optimism, realism, and kitchen wisdom (also known as common sense). For me, it is all about how to maximize a child's potential, and help a child become the best person they can be. So, as I say when first meeting a new client: "Let's get started and talk about your favorite topic of conversation, your child..."

The proceeds of the sale of this book and all future books will go to the "INA FUND," a charitable fund established by my office in 2015 in loving memory of Ina Hurwitz Cangiano, a woman who stood for the values of Integrity, kNowledge and Advocacy. The fund helps support special education in NYC—one child at a time.

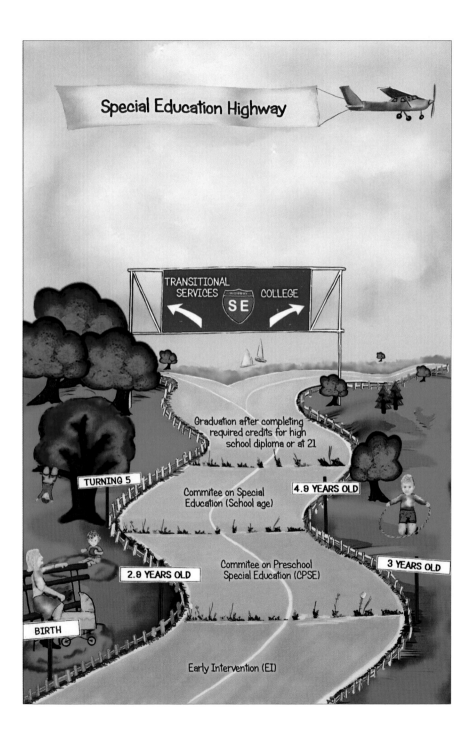

CHAPTER ONE

An Overview

Recently, I was sitting in the waiting room at a Committee on Special Education office and overheard this conversation:

"This was a hard turning-five; the child's been in EI, then CPSE with a dual rec of center and home-based. The diagnosis is PDD-NOS, which now means ASD. He's also ADHD, LD, SLI, and has SID. I wonder if he's really NI or CP? There are also some early signs of OCD and lots of ODD with dysgraphia, dyscalculia, and CAPD. Should we classify him SLI, ED, LD, ASD, OHI, or Multiple? For sure he needs lots of OT, PT, ST, and CO. If they parentally place, then we don't need to do an IEP and we can just do an IESP and issue a P-3. Then it goes to an agency for services—and I bet he gets nothing and then we'll have to issue RSAs. He doesn't belong in CTT, or SETSS; that wouldn't be enough. He's too smart for 12:1:1 or 12:1 and never 6:1:1. Maybe NEST? I left the IEP blank so he could get a P-1 or P-3 after a few more days; thank goodness for those Nickersons. Maybe we should just defer the case to CBST for NPS? Only thing is, what approved schools would be appropriate? I bet the parents want a Carter school or maybe Connor . . . maybe we should send an FNR? Also his mother said something about DAN as a medical alert—what's that?"

After listening to this conversation I didn't know whether to laugh or cry. If I hadn't spent the last 40 years of my life working in the field of special education, attending hundreds of Committee on Special Education (CSE) reviews, litigating at countless Impartial Hearings, and sitting with thousands of parents, I would have thought these people were speaking in tongues! I can only imagine what a parent who is first entering the system must feel like. Entering the world of the Department of Education (DOE) is like falling asleep at home and waking up in a foreign country without a cell phone. People around you are seemingly speaking the English language, but they are using words, phrases, terms, initials, abbreviations, and numbers that you've never heard. These strangers are all speaking about your child and making critical decisions about his or her life and future. The stakes are high and there is an urgency to master this new language, fully understand the process, and regain control of your child's life.

Unfortunately, most parents are not short-term visitors to special education. In fact, you have entered a country where, like it or not, you'll be living for the next several years, and sometimes indefinitely. Mastering the language of this "club" is the first part of your initiation process. The glossary at the end of this book, along with the overview in this chapter, should help parents learn the language and navigate the road ahead.

Before I address the turning-five process it is important for parents to have an overview of what I refer to as the "Special Education Highway." This highway can take you to three publicly funded programs created for children/students who meet age and eligibility requirements as a result of developmental, learning, or emotional problems. These programs are free of charge to parents and children.

The first stop on the Special Education Highway is the federal program known as **Early Intervention (EI)**. This program serves children from birth through age three. Referrals are generally made by a medical professional who is involved with the care or treatment of a child. A parent can also make their own referral to EI if they suspect that their young child has a developmental delay or an issue that is impeding development. The *location of residence of the child and family* determines which EI office is responsible for the evaluation and the coordination of services if the child is found eligible. Although services can continue until a child reaches the age of three, and in some instances even beyond their third birthday, once

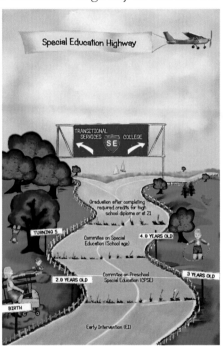

a child reaches the age of two years nine months (2.9) they cannot enter the EI system and must go directly to the next program on the highway: the Committee on Preschool Special Education (CPSE).

> TIP
> _____
>
> *If you believe that your infant or young toddler has a developmental delay, my advice is not to listen to nosey neighbors or your great Aunt Rose who tells you nothing is wrong. Even if your pediatrician tells you to wait and see, follow your instincts and run, don't walk, and have your child evaluated immediately. There is no harm in having an evaluation; these are not intrusive tests.*

An evaluation for an infant or young toddler can also be done privately by a developmental pediatrician. If you choose the route of a private developmental pediatrician and this doctor finds a delay, he or she will refer you to EI where the diagnosis and delay will be confirmed and services provided free of charge.

TIP

The Young Adult Institute (www.YAI.org), one of the city's best agencies providing services through EI, is a good place to get an orientation as to what is available through EI.

The second stop on the Special Education Highway is the **New York City Department of Education Committee on Preschool Special Education (CPSE)**. This program serves children ages two years nine months (2.9) through August of the calendar year in which they turn five. Admission to CPSE is determined first by a child's age and then by whether or not the child meets eligibility criteria. This can be confusing since CPSE serves children from as young as 2.9 to as old as five years nine months (5.9), meaning that sometimes there are similarly aged children who could be receiving services through EI or CPSE, or CPSE or CSE.

There are two groups of children that enter CPSE: (1) those that are receiving services through EI, and (2) those that are new and just entering the system. A new referral to CPSE can be made for a child from the age of 2.9 through four years nine months (4.9).

GROUP ONE - Children Receiving Services through Early Intervention

This group of children has several options. Hopefully a parent in this group has a knowledgeable service coordinator from EI who is guiding them through the transition from EI into CPSE. The EI coordinator generally attends the initial CPSE meeting with a parent in order to ensure continuity of service. A child who receives services through EI is entitled to have their EI services continue up until the day before their third birthday. A parent can opt to remain in EI and extend their child's services beyond their third birthday, but only under the following conditions: (1) For a child born between January 1st and August 31st, their parent can choose to extend EI services through August 31st. If this choice is made, CPSE services begin on September 1st; (2) For a child born between September 1st and December 31st, their parent can choose to extend EI through December 31st. If this choice is made, CPSE services begin on January 1st.

TIP
_____

The decision about when your child should leave EI and enter
CPSE is highly individualized, and a great deal of thought and
planning must be taken. To help make this decision, you can
consult with either an attorney or an advocate as your child
approaches the end of EI. At this consultation, you should secure
advice in preparation for your first CPSE meeting and understand
your options and the implications of each choice.

GROUP TWO - Children Entering CPSE Who Have Not Previously Received Services

The second group of children eligible for a CPSE evaluation and services are those that are already three years old, or approaching that age, and are not receiving services through EI. For this group of children there is generally a suspicion of a problem once the child has entered an early learning environment. The parent or a professional working with the child can make the referral.

I often hear about a child who begins in a typical preschool and whose parent receives a phone call early in the school year from the school director reporting delays in language development or problems with behavior regulation or peer relationships. The preschool director may be the first person to talk to the parent about a referral to the CPSE. Luckily, most preschool directors have familiarity with the CPSE process and can guide parents in the beginning stages.

TIP
_____

If your child's preschool is not making the referral to CPSE and
you suspect or recognize a problem, you should immediately
initiate the referral to CPSE. The first thing to do is to write a
referral letter to the chairperson of the CSE in the region where
you live. Be sure to make a copy of the referral letter to keep for
your records.

TIP
_____

If the teacher or director of your child's preschool tells you that
they can make the referral to the CPSE for you, I strongly
recommend you decline this offer and that you (the parent)
immediately send the referral letter.

TIP
_____

Whenever you send a referral letter or, for that matter, any letter
to the DOE, be sure to include your home address, date the letter,
and always send it certified mail, return receipt requested, or use

*Federal Express. Save a copy of the letter and the receipt. If you
choose to fax a letter, be sure to print a facsimile transmission
report which indicates the date and time the fax was sent and
received. Do not use a fax cover page; simply send the first page of
your letter so that the transmission report shows what was
received by the DOE. The bottom line is that you must have proof
of delivery in all correspondences! The time in which a district
must respond to your request for an evaluation or services is
legally governed.*

TIP

*Save the receipt of this certified letter, fax, or email and become
vigilant in ensuring that the referral is acted upon. If you are told
by someone at the CPSE that it will take many months to first get
to your case, do not accept this. This is against the law!*

RULE

*If a child is referred to the CPSE, it is the location of where the
child and family resides that determines which DOE office the
referral will go to.*

Due to the enormity of the children served by the DOE in New York
City, the 32 geographic districts are subdivided into 10 Regions.

TIP

*Refer to the chart "Where to Go," at the end of this chapter to
determine your district and region. If you are not sure of what
district/region you reside in either call 311 or visit the Department
of Education Web site (schools.nyc.gov).*

The third stop on the Special Education Highway is the **Committee on Special Education (CSE)**. This is also referred to as the "school-
age unit" of the CSE. For a child four years nine months (4.9) or older,
when there is suspicion of a problem impacting the child's education,
whether it is academic, language-based, social, emotional, or physical, a
free evaluation from the CSE is always available. If a child is found to be
eligible, then the child will be provided with an Individualized Education Program (IEP) or an Individualized Education Services Program
(IESP). In 2007 the DOE published a memorandum explaining the right
to an IESP when a parent chooses to place their child at a non-public
school at their own expense. This memo can be found at:
www.p12.nysed.gov/specialed/publications/policy/nonpublicparent.htm

An IESP is used as an alternative to an IEP when a parent places
their child in a mainstream or parochial nonpublic school at their own

How to Enter CPSE

Directly from Early Intervention

- Automatic referral
- Done with assistance from EI service coordinator

New Referrals

- Age 2.9 - 4.9
- Initiate with a letter to the CSE Chairperson

3 Choices of Time of CPSE entry

CHOICE 1: Can continue with EI until age 3

CHOICE 2: Born between Sept-Dec can start with CPSE early to get a preschool seat

CHOICE 3: Can extend EI past age 3

Born January 1 - August 31 can extend EI through August 31

Born September 1 - December 31 can extend EI through December 31

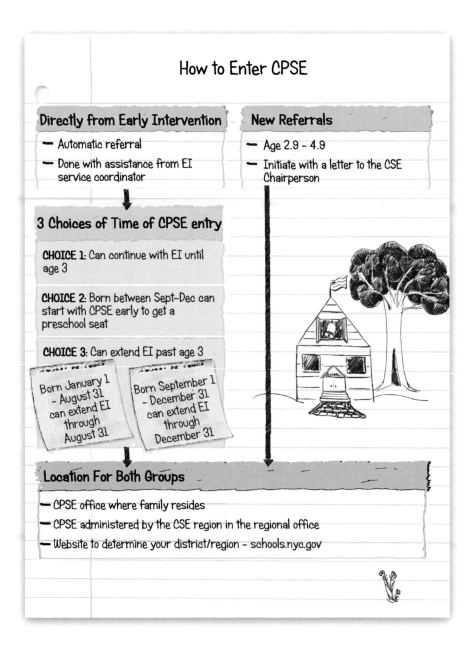

Location For Both Groups

- CPSE office where family resides
- CPSE administered by the CSE region in the regional office
- Website to determine your district/region - schools.nyc.gov

expense. An IESP will give a child comparable services at their nonpublic school, which means any of the related services or resource room or tutoring services. These services can be delivered by an agency contracted with the DOE and provided at the nonpublic school, in a provider's office, or in the child's home. If an agency is not available, then a voucher known as a Related Service Authorization (RSA) is issued.

> **TIP**
> _____
> *If you chose an IESP over an IEP there are serious implications. For example, if you chose an IESP you are not entitled to sue for tuition reimbursement.*

Eligibility for CSE services, either with an IEP or IESP, ends when the student receives a valid high school diploma or by the end of the school year in which the student turns twenty-one, whichever comes first.

A child who is already known to the CPSE as a result of being classified as a preschooler with a disability, and who receives services under the auspices of the CPSE, is automatically referred to the school-age unit of the CSE for a turning-five CSE review. There is nothing that a parent has to do to initiate this process.

> **TIP**
> _____
> *A parent must cooperate with their CSE. Agreeing and cooperating are not the same things. Cooperating means that you should keep all appointments, make your child available for any requested testing, and provide the CSE with requested forms as well as your own private evaluations. A parent should never disrupt the work and process of the CSE review team.*

There is another group of children who are not known to the CPSE but who, in the opinion of their parent, need to have an IEP and special education and/or related services for kindergarten. These children are similarly considered turning-five students. Their entry point is the school-age division of the CSE. In my opinion, the initial referral to the CSE should always be initiated by a parent by means of a letter addressed to the CSE/school district where the child and family reside. The referral letter must include the home address, be dated, and be sent certified mail or Federal Express with a return receipt requested or in any other manner in which receipt can be confirmed.

If a child is in a NYC public school kindergarten or higher grade and a parent wants the child to be evaluated by the CSE, or if the parent has a private evaluation and wants an IEP and special education program or services, then the parent should make a referral to the School Based Support Team (SBST) in the public school that the child attends.

If the child is in a private school, the referral should be made to the CSE where the private school is located.

The question of where to make the referral can be very confusing, so let's look at this example:

Kathy and Ronnie Smith live in Park Slope, Brooklyn, with their two children. This means their home school district is District 15/Region 8. Sam, their three-year-old son was born in April 2011. He attends a day care/preschool located near Kathy's office in Lower Manhattan, which is in District 2/Region 9. In September 2014, shortly after starting at this preschool, the director informed Kathy that Sam has language delays that impact on his behavior. The preschool director recommended contacting the CPSE in District 15/Region 8, the family's home region, for an evaluation. The evaluation for Sam was done over several days by a private agency that the CPSE contracted. Kathy was pleased with the quality of the evaluation, which resulted in Sam being eligible for classification as a "Preschooler with a Disability." After meeting eligibility criteria, the CPSE developed an IEP which recommended a Special Education Itinerant Teacher (SEIT), Speech Therapy (ST), and Occupational Therapy (OT). The CPSE coordinator at District 15/Region 8 did all the work. She found the SEIT and therapy providers, and arranged for them to provide their services at Sam's preschool.

RULE

Referrals for a CPSE evaluation always are made to the school district where the family resides.

Because Sam was born in April 2011, his preschool services come to an end in August 2016. In September 2016, Sam would be eligible to attend a school-age kindergarten program. Kathy and Ronnie visited their local public school in Brooklyn and observed the Integrated Co-Teaching (ICT) class as well as the self-contained 12:1:1 class. Neither program was right for Sam. His parents applied to, and Sam was accepted at, the Parkside School, located on the Upper West Side in District 3/Region 10. (This example is used solely for the purpose of helping readers understand jurisdiction, not the private school process, which is discussed in depth in Chapter Three.)

Because Sam and his family reside in District 15/Region 8, his Turning Five Review Meeting will be held in that region, regardless of the fact that his preschool is in another district/region or that the school his parents want him to attend is in an entirely different district/region.

RULE

All Turning Five Review Meetings occur in the district/region where the family resides, either at the family's local home-zoned public school, another nearby public school, or at the CSE main office.

In September 2016, the day Sam begins at the Parkside School, either at the recommendation of the CSE, or by his parents' choice and willingness to pay for the placement while they go through the process of seeking funding, the jurisdiction of his case shifts from Region 8 to Region 10. This means that as long as Sam attends a school in Region 10, like Parkside, all future CSE reviews will be held in Region 10, which is located on the Upper West Side of Manhattan.

TIP

At the end of this chapter are samples of draft letters that can be used to initiate a CPSE and CSE referral. Please modify these drafts and make your letter fact-specific to your child and your situation. Technically, all you have to do is give your child's name, date of birth, address, and write: "I am requesting a CSE or CPSE evaluation and review for my child." However, I prefer that the referral letter provides more facts and indicates what your concerns are and what you believe to be your child's issues and needs.

TIP

If you have a private evaluation or a report from a related service provider such as a speech, occupational, or physical therapist, these should be given to the CSE either as an enclosure in the initial referral letter or at your first meeting with the social worker from the DOE.

TIP

Even if you have sent copies of your private evaluation and other reports to the CSE in your referral letter, be sure to bring an extra copy of these to the actual review meeting. It is not uncommon for the CSE to misplace or not have these at your initial meeting.

TIP

In the sample letters you will note there is a sentence about giving consent for the CSE to speak with professionals and conduct any of their own assessments. I recommend including this sentence so that the CSE cannot argue that their compliance day begins later, when a parent signs consent forms.

Now that you have a preliminary overview of the three public programs available to children/students from birth through twenty-one, let's return to the subject of this book, the turning-five process.

The Calendar Year Rule

New York City insists on following what I have termed the "Calendar Year Rule":

RULE

A child is considered to be school-aged in September of the year in which he/she turns five. As a result of this rule, the child will no longer be eligible for special education programs and services through the jurisdiction of the CPSE come that September.

For example, all children born anytime during calendar year 2011 are "turning-five" students as of September 2016. Similarly, all children born anytime during calendar year 2012 are considered turning-five students in September 2017 and so on. This explains why, in NYC, there are kindergarten classrooms where there are four and five-year-old students sitting side-by-side. The rule is "turning five" not "being five." It is during the transition of leaving or aging out of the CPSE and entering CSE that the DOE will refer to your child as a "turning-five" student.

Let me give you an example of how the "Calendar Year Rule" works:

Sophie and Jack live next door to one another. Sophie was born on 1/1/11 at 12:01 a.m. while Jack was born on 12/31/11 at 11:30 p.m. They are chronologically a full year apart. On September 1, 2016, Sophie will be five years nine months old, and Jack will be four years nine months old. However, in NYC, they are both considered school-age, turning-five students. If Sophie and Jack were CPSE students and enrolled in either a center-based preschool program, or receiving SEIT and related services, both of their programs and services would come to a crashing halt at the end of August 2016. It is possible that Sophie and Jack could be placed in the same kindergarten class, regardless of their levels of maturity and development.

Difference Between Being Eligible and Being Required to Attend School

There is a significant difference between a child being eligible to attend school and being required to attend school. The term "compulsory education," refers to the legal requirement that a child must receive an education either at a school or by being properly home-schooled.

RULE
_____

In New York State compulsory education begins in September of the year in which the child turns six and ends when a child becomes sixteen years of age.

If a parent chooses to send their child to kindergarten in the year that the child turns five, a public school cannot deny entry into a kinder-garten placement on the grounds that it is not compulsory for the child to be in school. The compulsory education rule, as it exists today, gives parents the discretion to send their child to kindergarten but does not give equal discretion for the public schools to refuse a child entry.

The danger of not enrolling a child in kindergarten in September of the year they turn five is that the DOE is only obligated to give a turning -five child a kindergarten slot. So the following year, the DOE may or may not grant that child a kindergarten placement. Instead, they may offer a first grade placement. This concern does not apply to a child entering a private school. Private schools have discretion to set their own age requirements.

The hard and fast "Calendar Year Rule" leads to many questions and concerns. For example, a child may have been born prematurely and have had to spend the first three months of their life in a neonatal ICU; or a child may have developmental delays and is not ready to be in an all-day kindergarten in a large public school. Some children appear and behave as though they are much younger. Some children are not toilet trained, still nap in the afternoon, or are too immature and do not have the academic readiness skills needed for kindergarten. These are impor-tant concerns for a parent, but entirely irrelevant to the DOE, which adheres to the hard and fast "Calendar Year Rule," allowing for no flexibility.

Here is an example, based on a case that I handled many years ago, of how the Calendar Year Rule is unreasonable:

Shirley was adopted from a rural region of China before her first birthday. She was abandoned at an orphanage and there are no birth records. Given her low weight and obvious deprivations, it was impossible to determine the exact date of her birth. For passport and immigration purposes, her mother chose a birth date of December 20th. This was the birthday of the grandmother for whom the child was being named. Clearly, Shirley could have been given a birth date a month or even six weeks later. Her mother never anticipated the consequences of this decision. Shortly after Shirley was brought home to Brooklyn, it was determined that she had developmental delays, which was not surprising given her traumatic infancy. She immediately began receiving services through EI and then the CPSE.

Because Shirley's family lived in New York City, the Calendar Year Rule applied. Her mother was told by the CSE that Shirley would have to leave her thera-

Difference in Eligibility Requirements between Early Intervention, CPSE, and CSE

EARLY INTERVENTION

- 12 month delay in one or more functional areas

or

- 33 percent delay in one functional area

or

- 25 percent delay in each of two functional areas

or

- If standardized instruments are used during the evaluation process, a score of at least 15 standard deviation points below the mean in each of two functional areas

COMMITTEE ON PRESCHOOL SPECIAL EDUCATION

- 12 month delay in one or more functional areas

or

- 33 percent delay in one functional area

or

- 25 percent delay in each of two functional areas

COMMITTEE ON SPECIAL EDUCATION

- Must meet criteria for one of the 13 classifications recognized and defined by NYS Education Law

and

- Disability must impact on child's school performance

and

- Requires special education and/or related services

Committee on Special Education (CSE)

One Chairperson Oversees Two Branches

DIFFERENCES

PRESCHOOL CPSE	SCHOOL-AGE CSE
—CPSE Administrator assigned to help parents and remains with case	—No identified administrator or case manager
—All evaluations contracted to private agencies at no cost to parents (possibly changing to evaluations being done by school district)	—Evaluations done by CSE clinicians or privately at parents' expense
—CPSE Administrator finds and funds private "center-based" preschool	—No accessible placement officer
—CPSE Administrator arranges transportation to and from the preschool	—Private school placement difficult to obtain
—CPSE Administrator finds and funds private related services if recommended (including SEIT)	—Transportation to a private school difficult to obtain unless CSE recommends this
—Possible to receive a dual recommendation of a center-based and afterschool program (very difficult starting in 2013)	—No afterschool program
—One generic classification: "preschool student with a disability"	—Bound by Least Restrictive Environment (LRE) and Phase 2 of the new Initiative on Special Education
—Housed in Regional CSE office	—Must qualify for and receive one of 13 classifications
	—Review teams housed in local public schools

peutic special education preschool and go to a kindergarten class, based solely on her date of birth as it appeared on her birth certificate. Shirley was tiny, not toilet trained, still napped in the afternoon, needed a stroller, and presented as a much younger toddler without any of the basic pre-academic skills expected of a child entering kindergarten.

I accompanied Shirley's mother to the Turning Five Review Meeting, which in those days was held at the district office. We tried to dispute the Calendar Year Rule as being arbitrary and capricious, not to mention illogical. We submitted letters from the child's preschool, her therapists, and the adoption agency, as well as a detailed report from a renowned developmental pediatrician who specialized in foreign adoptions. Every person on the review team in principle agreed with us, including all the representatives from the school district. Nonetheless, we were told that the CSE could not recommend another year of preschool because of the official birth date that appeared on the child's records.

Fortunately for Shirley, we were able to get her what she needed, which was another year of preschool and preschool services. This happened as a result of an Impartial Hearing. At the hearing I invoked a statutory provision in the IDEA called *Stay Put*. Stay Put is also referred to as "preschool pendency." We have been using this provision for hundreds of children over the last twenty plus years, because of its important value. (See Chapter Four to understand the legal provision of Stay Put/Pendency.)

TIP

I will reiterate these words of warning several times: If you are thinking of having your turning-five child remain in preschool with a CPSE IEP instead of entering kindergarten, do not discuss this at a CSE meeting or with staff from the DOE without first consulting with an attorney who practices in this area of law and who has done pendency hearings. The word "pendency" implies an impending lawsuit and should not be how you start a relationship with your CSE.

Whether to Use an Attorney or Advocate

I am frequently asked whether a parent should hire an attorney or advocate and what the differences are. Before hiring any professional to help you understand this process, I strongly encourage that parents network with other parents who are or have been in a similar situation. Most parents are more than willing to share information, give guidance, make suggestions, and point others in the right direction. If you are still feeling overwhelmed and frightened by the process and what lies ahead of you, then it is time to hire or at least consult with a professional.

If a parent can afford to do so, I suggest an initial consultation meeting with either an attorney who specializes in this area of law or a seasoned lay advocate. Come prepared for that meeting with your own agenda and questions. Use that hour to identify and discuss the issues, problems, and concerns. Not all consultations result in retaining the attorney or advocate. However, a thorough consultation will provide you with an understanding of your options. Knowledge means empowerment and knowing that there is an attorney behind you will help those sleepless nights.

TIP

There is an advocate who provides free seminars throughout the year in order to help parents understand and navigate the turning-five process. Be sure to attend one of these. Visit: www.nyspecialneeds.com.

There is a huge difference between an attorney and a lay advocate. An advocate can help a parent understand the system and is familiar with private schools and their admission process. An attorney whose specialty is special education law can serve as both an attorney and advocate. The profession of law teaches and requires attorneys to be zealous advocates on behalf of their clients. The distinguishing factor between an attorney and a lay advocate is the attorney's educational background, knowledge and application of the law to the facts of the case. Many attorneys practicing in the area of special education law have dual degrees in social work, psychology, or special education.

There are several factors to consider when choosing an attorney. The attorney must have expertise representing special education children and their parents at CSE review meetings, must be able to file for a due process Impartial Hearing and serve as a litigator at the hearing. Additionally this attorney should have experience filing for (prosecuting) and answering (defending) appeals against the New York State Department of Education at the Office of State Review and in United States Federal Courts.

TIP

Whatever you do, do not use your cousin Vinnie, who does real estate closings or wills and took a continuing education course in special education law. If you needed open heart surgery, you would not use a dermatologist.

There are several advocates in New York City, some of whom have decades of experience in negotiating and dealing with the DOE and understanding the ins and outs of this complex bureaucracy. An advocate is sometimes referred to as a "lay advocate" because they are not required to have any degree or credentials, just a passion and knowledge about the programs and services that are available. The terms "advocate" and "lay advocate" can be used interchangeably. Most advocates are motivated to enter this field because of their own experiences pertaining to their child or relative. As a result, they want to help other parents navigate through the system. An advocate's experience as a parent has value, and an advocate can help other parents who are beginning the process. Most of the NYC advocates focus on helping parents secure private school admission and are familiar with the various private special education schools and their admissions directors.

There is a further distinction between an advocate and an educational consultant. An educational consultant typically has a professional degree and significant experience in special education. They understand, from a clinical perspective, the needs of the child as well as which programs and services can best meet a specific child's needs. Because of their backgrounds, consultants are often called upon as expert witnesses at Impartial Hearings and must be willing to testify if a case proceeds to an Impartial Hearing. Most attorneys in this field have lists of educational consultants that they refer to.

An advocate or educational consultant can help guide a parent through the turning-five process. However, understand that if you use such a person it does not necessarily eliminate the need for an attorney. If you are seeking tuition reimbursement, pendency, or funding for a private school placement, you will most likely have to sue or threaten to sue your district at an Impartial Hearing. This should be done by an attorney.

SAMPLE LETTER 1

To Initiate a CPSE Referral
(Keep in mind that this is just a draft and should be customized to fit your unique set of facts and issues.)

Home Address
Date

Chairperson
CSE Region ___
Address
Sent via Certified Mail Return Receipt
RE: (Child's name and date of birth)

Dear Chairperson:

My son Jack is currently attending ABC Preschool, located at XYZ. At the suggestion of (name), the director of this preschool, we are writing to request an evaluation and review by the CPSE. Jack has been reported as having language delays as well as some difficulties with social interactions.

This letter will serve as my consent for you or someone from your offices to speak with the preschool director and to conduct evaluations and assessments as you deem necessary. This letter will also serve as my consent to electronic communication.

Thank you, and I look forward to hearing from you. I request that this process begins as soon as possible.

Very truly yours,

_____
Parent(s)
Cell phone number
Email

SAMPLE LETTER 2

To Initiate a CSE Referral
(Keep in mind that this is just a draft and should be customized to fit your unique set of facts and issues.)

Home Address
Date

Chairperson
CSE Region ___
Address
Sent via Certified Mail Return Receipt
RE: (Child's name and date of birth)

Dear Chairperson:

I am requesting a CSE review for my child. As you can see from my child's birth date, he/she will turn five this coming school year. My child currently attends ABC Preschool, located at XYZ. At the suggestion of the preschool director I had him/her privately evaluated by Dr. Learned. Enclosed is a copy of this report. As you can see from the findings, Dr. Learned is recommending that my child receive an IEP and be recommended for a special education program and services.

This letter will serve as my consent for your offices to contact the preschool director, to conduct any and all assessments, evaluations, or observations that you deem necessary, and to speak with the private evaluator whose name and contact information appears on the enclosed report. This letter will also serve as my consent to electronic communication.

Thank you.

Very truly yours,

_____
Parent(s)
Cell phone number
Email

CSE Regions and Districts

CSE 1	DISTRICT	7, 9, 10	CONTACT	Steven Birkland
	ADDRESS	One Fordham Plaza, 7th Flr.	PHONE/FAX	P: (718) 329-8001
		Bronx, NY 10458		F: (718) 741-7928, (718) 741-7929
CSE 2	DISTRICT	8, 11, 12	CONTACT	Tricia DeVito
	ADDRESS	3450 East Tremont Ave., 2nd Flr.	PHONE/FAX	P: (718) 794-7429 Español:
		Bronx, NY 10465		F: (718) 794-7445 (718) 794-7490
CSE 3	DISTRICT	25, 26	CONTACT	Esther Morell
	ADDRESS	30-48 Linden Place	PHONE/FAX	P: (718) 281-3461
		Flushing, NY 11354		F: (718) 281-3478
	DISTRICT	28, 29	CONTACT	Esther Morell
	ADDRESS	90-27 Sutphin Boulevard	PHONE/FAX	P: (718) 557-2553
		Jamaica, NY 11435		F: (718) 557-2620, (718) 557-2510
CSE 4	DISTRICT	24, 30	CONTACT	Chris Cinicola
	ADDRESS	28-11 Queens Plaza N., 5th Flr.	PHONE/FAX	P: (718) 391-8405
		Long Island City, NY 11101		F: (718) 391-8556
	DISTRICT	27	CONTACT	Chris Cinicola
	ADDRESS	Satellite Office, 82-01 Rockaway	PHONE/FAX	P: (718) 642-5715
		Blvd., 2nd Flr., Ozone Park, NY 11416		F: (718) 642-5891
CSE 5	DISTRICT	19, 23, 32	CONTACT	Geraldine Beauvil
	ADDRESS	1665 St. Marks Avenue	PHONE/FAX	P: (718) 240-3557, (718) 240-3558
		Brooklyn, NY 11233		F: (718) 240-3555
CSE 6	DISTRICT	17, 18, 22	CONTACT	Arlene Rosenstock
	ADDRESS	5619 Flatlands Avenue	PHONE/FAX	P: (718) 968-6200
		Brooklyn, NY 11234		F: (718) 968-6253
CSE 7	DISTRICT	20, 21	CONTACT	Amine Haddad
	ADDRESS	415 89th Street	PHONE/FAX	P: (718) 759-4900
		Brooklyn, NY 11209		F: (718) 759-4970
	DISTRICT	31	CONTACT	Amine Haddad
	ADDRESS	715 Ocean Terrace, Building A	PHONE/FAX	P: (718) 420-5700
		Staten Island, NY 11209		F: (718) 420-5787
CSE 8	DISTRICT	13, 14, 15, 16	CONTACT	Cherry Kang
	ADDRESS	131 Livingston Street, 4th Flr.	PHONE/FAX	P: (718) 935-4900
		Brooklyn, NY 11201		F: (718) 935-5167
CSE 9	DISTRICT	1, 2, 4	CONTACT	Jennifer Lozano-Luna
	ADDRESS	333 7th Avenue, 4th Flr.	PHONE/FAX	P: (917) 339-1600
		New York, NY 10001		F: (917) 339-1450
CSE 10	DISTRICT	3, 5, 6	CONTACT	Jane O'Connor
	ADDRESS	388 West 125th Street	PHONE/FAX	P: (212) 342-8300
		New York, NY 10027		F: (212) 342-8427
CHARTER SCHOOLS	DISTRICT	ALL	CONTACT	Mariana Sundi
	ADDRESS	One Fordham Plaza, 7th Flr.	PHONE/FAX	P: (718) 320-8001
		Bronx, NY 10458		F: (718) 741-7928

CHAPTER TWO

Getting Started

Finally, it has all come together; your little boy Adam is happy in his preschool and making notable progress in all areas of development. He leaves home every morning with a big smile and returns home just as happy. With the help of your Early Intervention (EI) coordinator, when he transitioned from EI into the Committee on Preschool Special Education (CPSE), you were able to get the same level of home services. The following year, when Adam was four, your CPSE coordinator found him a full-day special education preschool which the DOE entirely funded, along with door -to-door busing in a small minibus. The CPSE referred to the preschool as a center-based program.

Adam wasn't making as much progress as you and the preschool had hoped for. But, with some strong advocacy, the support of the preschool, and well prepared reports, you were able to add seven hours of an after-school program consisting of a Special Education Itinerant Teacher (SEIT), Speech Therapy (ST), and Occupational Therapy (OT). Initially it felt like a treasure hunt, finding providers and coordinating everyone's schedule. But your hard work has paid off because Adam's progress is remarkable. Every person who knows him comments on his improvement. Things are humming along and you are feeling hopeful and optimistic.

What worries you is that this wonderful center-based and home program will soon come to a crashing halt. Adam was born in 2011 and in the early spring of 2016, he will have a turning-five CSE review. By September 2016, Adam will be expected to enter a school-age kindergarten program if you choose to use the public schools. The generosity and helpfulness from the CPSE will be over. The days of dealing with one DOE administrator who assists in organizing services and finding the right program and providers are gone. You have been repeatedly told that under no circumstances will Adam receive an after-school program through the CSE.

Equally upsetting is that your local home-zoned public school is not appropriate for Adam. It is far too large, overwhelming, and all his therapists told you that placing him there would put him at risk for regression. You have heard about an outstanding public school program in Williamsburg, Brooklyn close to your home called NEST. After researching this program you found out that not only is it hard to get into, but in order to qualify Adam would have to meet the criteria for an Autistic Spectrum Disorder diagnosis and be classified as ASD. This wouldn't be an option. You know about private special education schools, but these schools are difficult to get into, the cost is prohibitive, and it generally involves a lawsuit. The whole process sounds daunting. There are days you look at Adam, convinced that he is not ready to leave his

Turning 5 Process - An Overview

BEFORE THE TURNING 5 REVIEW MEETING

Referral
- Automatic if child is known to the CSE
- By parental referral with a certified letter

Consent
- Parents must give consent to the process

Evaluations and Updates
- Can be done privately at parent's expense
- Can be done by CSE staff at no expense
- Can be a combination of both

Notice of the Meeting
- Must be in writing, sent to parents with date, time, place of meeting

AT THE TURNING 5 REVIEW MEETING

Required Membership
- The Parent(s)
- School Pyschologist
- District Representative
- Special Education Teacher
- General Education Teacher

Optional Membership
- Parent Member
- Physician Member

Three Purposes of Turning 5 Meetings
- Determine eligibility and classification
- Develop an Individualized Education Program (IEP)
- Make a Program Recommendation

Three Considerations
- Least Restrictive Environment
- Phase 2 of the New Initiative
- NYS Continuum

AFTER THE TURNING 5 REVIEW MEETING

Final Notice of Recommendation

Visit the Actual Placement

Accept the Public School Placement

Reject the Public School Placement

Private School

Pendency

preschool. You've heard the term "pendency," but have no idea what this means or what it involves. Your anxiety is mounting.

If any of this sounds familiar . . . read on.

All turning-five students have four broad categories of options available to them for their kindergarten year:

I. **PUBLIC SCHOOL PROGRAMS:** Generally, this means either an Integrated Co-Teaching Class (ICT, or sometimes still referred to as a CTT); a Self-Contained Class in a local Community School (usually a 12:1:1 or a 12:1 class) or a District 75 Program, which is also referred to as a Special Class in a Specialized School (class sizes for District 75 programs are: 12:1:1, 8:1:1, 6:1:1 or 12:1:4). The NEST program is a small ICT class for high-functioning children on the Autism Spectrum that is housed in general education schools. The Intensive Kindergarten (Intensive K) program is a class of six children, all classified as ASD, also housed in general education schools. It has been determined that Intensive K students could be eligible for the NEST program but they need another year of intensive services before being able to enter NEST.

For some families the option of a public school program will mean moving to a suburban school district.

Options for All Turning Five Students

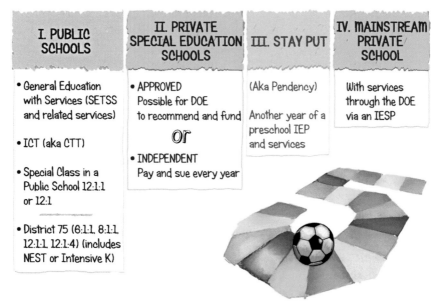

I. PUBLIC SCHOOLS	II. PRIVATE SPECIAL EDUCATION SCHOOLS	III. STAY PUT	IV. MAINSTREAM PRIVATE SCHOOL
• General Education with Services (SETSS and related services)	• APPROVED Possible for DOE to recommend and fund **or** • INDEPENDENT Pay and sue every year	(Aka Pendency) Another year of a preschool IEP and services	With services through the DOE via an IESP
• ICT (aka CTT)			
• Special Class in a Public School 12:1:1 or 12:1			
• District 75 (6:1:1, 8:1:1, 12:1:1, 12:1:4) (includes NEST or Intensive K)			

II. **PRIVATE SPECIAL EDUCATION SCHOOL:** There are two categories of private special education schools: Approved and Independent. (See Chapter Three)

III. **PENDENCY:** While a parent is disputing an issue concerning their child's IEP and/or placement recommendation, the last-agreed-to IEP shall govern and be funded by the school district. In practice, this permits another year of preschool but only when certain conditions are met. (See Chapter Four)

IV. **MAINSTREAM PRIVATE SCHOOL:** Here parents are responsible for paying the tuition, however, their child can receive an IESP and receive "comparable" services from the DOE at no charge. These services include SETSS (resource room) and/or related services (Speech, Occupational and Physical Therapies, and Counseling).

In the Beginning...

For a child who is already known to the CPSE, during the fall of their final year in preschool, the parent will be notified by mail that the CPSE has referred the child to the school-aged unit of the CSE. This notification letter is the official start of the turning-five process.

Accompanying this notice of referral, or sometimes in a second letter sent shortly thereafter, a parent is asked to complete and return the following forms: (1) Consent for Reevaluation; (2) Authorization of Release of Health Information Pursuant to HIPAA; (3) Request for Medical Accommodation (if applicable); (4) Parent Survey; (5) Medical Form labeled "section to be completed by Doctor"; (6) Contact Sheet.

> TIP
>
> *Districts and schools are not consistent in materials they send to parents. If something was not included in your initial letter or if you do not receive a letter at all, do not panic. In certain situations the DOE's inefficiency can be helpful in achieving a parent's desired outcome.*

A school psychologist or a school social worker from the local home-zoned public school or a nearby neighborhood school will be identified as the person in charge of your child's case. This person will gather materials, schedule appointments, and help move the process along, assuring that the CSE conducts a timely Turning Five Review Meeting.

> TIP
>
> *You should keep a detailed journal or diary. The entire CSE process is far more complicated than your experience with the*

CPSE. There are more players involved and different layers of bureaucracy. There is also a greater likelihood that you can find yourself in an adversarial position with your school district and wind up at an Impartial Hearing. Keeping a contemporaneous and detailed journal concerning all mailings, meetings, and conversations, can prove to be invaluable. Date all of your journal entries summarizing all of your conversations.

TIP

Along with your journal, I advise purchasing an accordion file organized by months. In this file, save all mail and correspondences with any branch of the DOE, including emails. Make a copy of everything you receive from the DOE and keep the envelope in which letters or forms arrive. Keeping the envelope in which mail arrives is very important. Every year, there are several cases seeking private school funding that have been won solely because we can prove a late arrival of a placement notice.

TIP

It is essential that you sign the consent form and return a completed physical exam form. Since it can take weeks or months to get the physical exam form completed by your pediatrician, I recommend sending the consent form first and then the physical exam. These forms are returned to the person the DOE named on this form. This should all be noted in your journal.

TIP

At all times you must fully cooperate with the district. However, this does not mean that you have to do their job.

TIP

When corresponding with the CSE for any matter whatsoever, always include your child's nine-digit New York City identification number, which is sometimes referred to as an "OSIS" number or a Local ID.

TIP
___

*Send all correspondences (including the signed consent form) to the
CSE by certified mail (Federal Express is also acceptable), return
receipt requested, and save all receipts. Be sure to make a copy of
whatever you send to the CSE. This includes copying all material
when returning the consent form and when sending any reports
or evaluations.*

TIP
___

*Some parents choose to hand deliver the consent form to their
home-zoned school. This is a good idea as it gives you another
opportunity to visit your home-zoned school. Be sure to include
notes from this drop off in your journal. However, most parents do
not have the flexibility in their schedules to do this, and it is
perfectly acceptable to mail these materials back. If you choose to
hand deliver be sure to get an acknowledgement in writing from the
person who receives the forms. Also, always sign in at the front
entry desk.*

After receiving the notification letter from the CSE, most districts
send an invitation to attend an orientation meeting which is generally
held at the district office. The purpose of this meeting is to explain the
turning-five process from the DOE's perspective.

TIP
___

*Although the orientation meeting is not mandatory, I strongly
advise attending it. At this meeting keep a low profile; stay off the
radar. Listen to what is being said and take notes in your journal.
You can ask a question, but do not become the squeaky wheel.*

TIP
___

*Kindergarten registration at local public schools generally begins
in early January. Starting in 2014, registration for kindergarten is
done online and is referred to as "Kindergarten Connect." For
most parents I suggest registering their child at their local home-
zoned elementary school, regardless of whether you are applying to
private schools. The kindergarten admission process is new and
permits parents to apply not only to their home-zoned school, but
also to other schools of interest. If you have an interest in a school
outside of your immediate catchment area, apply to this school as
well and make contact with the principal. However, the popular*

schools will rarely accept a student who does not reside within their catchment area.

TIP

If you have an older child who attends a public school outside of your immediate catchment area and this is a school that you would consider for your turning-five child, contact the principal and try to get a sibling variance for your child.

TIP

Visit as many of the highly regarded public school kindergarten programs as you can. The purpose of visiting these schools is to become an "educated consumer." If down the road you are going to be arguing for a private school placement, the fact that you visited several public schools will lend credibility to your position that the public school programs cannot meet your child's needs. You might be pleasantly surprised and actually want to try one of the public school programs.

TIP

During your visit to any public schools ask to see the different types of classes and services that are available to special education students. Take notes of all of your visits and write down the names and positions of the people with whom you meet. Always make an entry in your journal of the exact date and time that you visited the school.

TIP

If you suspect that your child will be recommended to a District 75 Program, try and visit some of the placement sites within District 75. A list of schools is available on the DOE website: schools.nyc.gov/Academics/SpecialEducation/D75/AboutD75/ Schools.htm

TIP

Most public schools do not allow walk-in visits. They generally have orientation meetings and tours for incoming kindergarten parents. There is a parent coordinator at each school who will assist in scheduling. If you cannot reach this person by telephone it is perfectly acceptable to go to the school.

What Happens in Preparation for the Turning Five Review Meeting?

Social History

At some point in the late winter or early spring, a social worker from the home-zoned school will contact the parent or guardian to conduct a "social history." This interview can be done over the telephone or in person. It can be completed by either of the child's parents or guardians, or both. Many parents have had a social history completed as part of previous evaluations and are familiar with what will be asked at this interview. The social history interview generally lasts for an hour. The DOE representative will ask questions about the child's birth and early history, the family's home life, and what the parent perceives as the child's issues and needs.

During the social history interview a DOE publication entitled *A Parent's Guide to Special Education Services for School-Age Children* will be provided. In some instances, the social worker will actually discuss the contents of this document and explain what rights a parent has. It is important that you read this publication, which is available on-line at: *www.p.12.nysed.gov/specialed/publications/policy/parentguide.htm*

TIP

*Occasionally the DOE professional who is conducting the social history will ask you a question regarding what you think your child's needs are and what type of kindergarten placement you believe will be appropriate. If you are asked this question, be truthful, but remember, in this situation **less is more**. It is perfectly acceptable to answer: "I don't know … I am exploring all options," or "I know my child needs a small class in a highly specialized school, and I am open to your suggestions," or "I think that my child is not ready for an academic kindergarten program and needs another year of preschool." I often suggest the strategy of turning the question around and asking the DOE representative: "What do you think my child needs?" or "What do other parents in my situation do?"*

TIP

*Whatever you do, **NEVER** say, "I want a year of pendency." Instead, what you can say is: "I do not think my child is ready to enter a school-age program, and I believe he needs another year of preschool." (See Chapter Four)*

How to Prepare for a Turning 5 Review

WHAT THE SCHOOL DISTRICT DOES	WHAT THE PARENT SHOULD DO
✓ Send notice that child's case is referred to CSE with consent form.	✓ Sign and return consent form.
✓ Provide parents with health examination form that must be completed.	✓ Complete and return a health examination form (physician must do this).
✓ Conduct a social history with parent.	✓ Attend CSE open house.
✓ Review the child's entire file.	✓ Visit public school programs.
✓ Gather providers and teacher updates, which sometimes includes conversations with the professionals.	✓ Observe special education classes in public schools.
✓ Conduct a structured classroom observation.	✓ In fall, visit private special education schools that might be appropriate for the child.
✓ Send notice of the date, time, and place of the Turning Five meeting.	✓ If necessary have a private evaluation – do this in the early fall of your child's last year of preschool.
	✓ After having your attorney review your private evaluation, send it to the CSE.
	✓ Keep a journal of all conversatons and interactions with the CSE.
	✓ Save a copy of all correspondence with DOE.
	✓ Ask to see all reports done by CSE teachers, providers prior to the Turning Five meetings.
	✓ If possible, review any and all reports being sent to the DOE before they are actually sent.
	✓ All correspondences with the CSE from the parent should be in writing – either by email or certified mail.

TIP
_____

*Whatever you do, **NEVER** say, "I have no intention of sending my child to a public school and I will only consider placement in a private school." Instead, what you can say is: "My child's needs are very complex and from what I have seen, a large public school program will be unable to meet his needs. Are there any smaller public schools that I can take a look at?"*

TIP
_____

__ALWAYS__ say, "I am completely open to consider any and all programs and placements that the DOE or the professionals in my child's life believe to be appropriate for my child. I want to explore all available options in order to make the right decision and find my child an appropriate program." Maintain this position throughout all of your dealings with the DOE now and forever!

TIP
_____

If you have a private evaluation that you believe is accurate, provide this to the person who is conducting the social history. If you are in the process of having the private evaluation done, inform the DOE representative of this fact and ask for a card or address so you can send the report to the representative when it is completed. If you are working with an attorney or advocate, ask this person to review the private evaluation before you send it to the DOE.

TIP
_____

As with every conversation you have with the DOE, go home and write a journal entry, which should include the date, time, place of the meeting along with the name of the person with whom you met. Write specific details of what was discussed. It is best to do this as soon as possible while the conversation is fresh in your memory. Be as detailed and specific as you can. It is better to have too much information than too little.

Observation

An observation of a child by a DOE representative is a required as part of the turning-five assessment process. This is supposed to be done prior to the Turning Five Review Meeting and a written observation report should be available to the parent. If a child is in a center-based special education preschool or a typical mainstream preschool with a SEIT, someone from the CSE will go to the school, observe the child in the classroom, and interview the teacher, SEIT, and anyone else working with the child. A parent does not have a right to know the exact date that the CSE is coming to the school. Once a parent signs the broad consent form at the start of the turning-five process they have given consent for this observation and any other assessment.

TIP

You have a right to review the report generated from the observation before the Turning Five Review Meeting. If you know for sure that the CSE did an observation, then you can ask to see this report before the actual Turning Five Review Meeting.

TIP

The preschool should know beforehand when the CSE representative will be coming to do this observation, and you can ask your school to keep you informed.

TIP

If the CSE has not done an observation, discuss this with your attorney or advocate before taking any action. In some instances the failure to do an observation can help your case.

Review of File

In preparation for the Turning Five review, the psychologist or social worker from the School Based Support Team (SBST) at the local public school will review the child's file to determine if the clinical information is current. For a child who is known to the CPSE, the CSE generally does not conduct new evaluations or do new testing. It is customary for the CSE to rely upon earlier evaluations done when the child entered CPSE or upon any private evaluations submitted by the parent. The reasoning behind why the DOE does not do new evaluations as part of the turning-five process is because the law only requires school districts to re-evaluate classified students once every three years. For a turning-five child there had to have been a comprehensive evaluation as part of the admission process to the CPSE, which was always done less than three years before the Turning Five Review Meeting. The CSE will request updated progress reports from teachers and related service providers. This information will be used at the CSE review meeting to determine eligibility, classification, program recommendation, as well as to create the IEP goals.

TIP

The progress reports prepared by your child's SEIT and/or classroom teacher are very important and will be heavily relied upon at the Turning Five Review Meeting. It is a good idea for you to review these reports before they are sent to the CSE. It is important that there be consistency amongst the professionals working with your child as to what they believe is an appropriate recommendation for the upcoming school year.

Evaluations and Updates

In most turning-five cases the CSE does not conduct new evaluations and relies on subjective teacher and therapist reports. This lack of a current evaluation by the CSE does not mean that a parent should not have their child privately evaluated. Because of the great importance of a private evaluation at this juncture in a child's life and educational career, I have devoted an entire chapter to this subject (See Chapter Six). In spite of the DOE's policy, if a parent decides that they want an evaluation done by the CSE prior to their child's Turning Five Review Meeting *and* the most recent evaluation is more than one year old but less than three years old, a parent can request, in writing, that an evaluation be done by the CSE, and the CSE is then obligated to do it.

TIP

Asking the CSE to do current evaluations can have strategic value for a parent. However, this request has to be part of a larger plan.

TIP

If you are applying for admission to a private special education school, your child will need a current psycho-educational or neuropsychological evaluation. In these instances I would only use private evaluations.

TIP

If you are considering another year of preschool you will need to at the very least consult with a private psychologist/ neuropsychologist.

TIP

I cannot emphasize enough the importance of having your private evaluation reviewed by your attorney or advocate before submitting it to the CSE.

Private School Options

If parents believe that their child might need a private school placement, they should be exploring this option at the same time that they are exploring public school programs. Most parents start going on tours of private schools in October of the year prior to entry, and they have private evaluations scheduled to begin around the same time.

Many of the private special education schools schedule open houses/tours during the fall and early winter. Appointments for these tours are necessary and space is limited. Try to go on as many tours as possible and go sooner, rather than later. A tour of a private school is suggested, but if a parent has not visited a school, this does not mean that they cannot apply for admission.

TIP

Get applications for all the private schools that you are interested in and submit the applications with the required evaluations and progress reports as early as possible. Many schools have deadlines for submission of the applications and it is important that you adhere to these deadlines. Each school follows its own timetable; be sure you know what that is.

TIP

If a private school requires a current psycho-educational or neuropsychological evaluation as part of its admission application, have this done in the early fall and make sure it is ready no later than December 1st. It is best to find a private evaluator that you want to use and schedule an appointment for September or October. Some evaluators get booked very early and you may have to wait up to six months for an appointment, so call the evaluator in the spring for an appointment for the following fall. Be sure to tell this evaluator that you will need the final report by November so it can be reviewed and ready for December. If you cannot do this by the early fall, it is perfectly acceptable to do this later in the year, but it limits your being in the first batch of applicants.

TIP

Many private schools have lists of psychologists who they recommend as evaluators. Ask private schools for this list as it is worth using an evaluator who appears on several school lists. If there is a particular school that you want and the evaluator that you are planning to use is not on their list, specifically ask the evaluator if he or she has any familiarity with the school and ask the school if they know the evaluator.

Notice of the Meeting

In the spring preceding a child's scheduled entry into kindergarten, a parent will receive a written notice from the CSE scheduling the Turning Five Review Meeting. The notice must be in a parent's possession five (5) working days prior to the meeting, allowing time to arrange a parent's schedule in order to be present at the meeting. This meeting will take place at a parent's local home-zoned public school, another nearby public school, or the CSE Regional office.

> TIP
> ───────────────────────────────────
> *It is critical that you attend the Turning Five Review Meeting in person even if you think that you are not going to use any CSE services or programs. If you have a legitimate reason to postpone this meeting, immediately call the contact person, tell them your reason, and ask for an alternate date.*

> TIP
> ───────────────────────────────────
> *Do not delay unnecessarily. Be prepared for this meeting and let's get started!*

By the time a parent receives notice of the review meeting, they have met with a social worker or psychologist for a social history; the child should have been observed; teacher/provider updates will have been submitted to the CSE; and, if the child was privately tested, the report should have been submitted to the DOE.

> TIP
> ───────────────────────────────────
> *A parent should have visited public and private school programs at this point.*

> TIP
> ───────────────────────────────────
> *Before your Turning Five Review Meeting, request a copy of any DOE observation or other possible evaluations that the DOE did in the months leading up to this meeting. Ask to see everything that the CSE review team will be relying on at this meeting. Although the DOE does not automatically send this material, you have an absolute right to these reports and evaluations in advance of the meeting.*

> TIP
> ───────────────────────────────────
> *If you have trouble getting a copy of these reports, remind the CSE that on page six of the DOE publication, "Kindergarten: An Orientation Guide for Families of Students with Disabilities," this is listed as one of a parent's "rights." It is important to receive this*

*material in advance of the meeting so that you can use it to
effectively advocate for your child. For example, if all the reports
indicate that your child needs daily individual speech therapy for
45 minutes and the CSE determines that all they will provide are
three 30-minute sessions, two of which are in a group, these reports
are your best ammunition. Or, if every report recommends a small
self-contained class and the CSE recommends an ICT class, again,
you have ammunition (supporting documentation) to disagree
with their determination.*

TIP

*Even if you have already submitted your private evaluations to the
CSE, be sure to make extra copies and bring this to the Turning
Five Review Meeting.*

By the time that the Turning Five Review Meeting is scheduled, a parent should have a definite idea as to what the appropriate program or placement is for their child and, specifically, where they want the child to be in September.

TIP

*If your child has been accepted into a private special education
school, or if you are looking to repeat preschool, the stakes are high
and you must be working with an attorney who will answer your
emails and respond to your concerns and prepare you for this meeting.*

If for some reason a child's case has fallen through the cracks and by the late spring the parent has not received notice of the Turning Five Review Meeting, (depending on what the parent's plans are for September) there are several ways to deal with this. If a parent wants a public school program, they must actively pursue getting the review meeting by going to the public school that they were accepted to through Kindergarten Connect. If a parent is trying for a private school placement, or another year of a preschool program, they must immediately contact their attorney and follow the advice given. Failure to hold a meeting when the CSE knew or should have known of the need for such a meeting is a significant procedural error and can result in funding of a private school placement.

Who will be at the Turning Five Review Meeting?

The written notice for your meeting should include the date, time, and place of the meeting, as well as a list of the people who will participate.

The mandatory members for this meeting are:

- **Parents**
- **General Education Teacher,** who is, or may be, responsible for implementing the IEP (if the child will be attending a general education environment).
- **School Psychologist**
- **District Representative** (can be the school psychologist), who is the person with knowledge of the programs and services available.
- **Special Education Teacher,** who is, or may be, responsible for implementing the IEP.

The optional members for this meeting are:

- **Physician Member,** if requested, in writing, by a parent 72 hours in advance of the CSE review meeting.
- **Parent Member,** if requested, in writing, by a parent 72 hours in advance of the CSE review meeting. A "parent member" does not mean the child's own parent. The parent member is a person who resides in the district, has a child enrolled in special education, and is present to assist the parents through the process.

> ### TIP
> *I recommend that your SEIT and/or the special education teacher from your child's center-based preschool attend this meeting with you. These people can attend by phone if that is what their schedules permit. No matter the manner in which they attend, their involvement and participation in the meeting is very important.*

> ### TIP
> *If your SEIT or special education teacher is participating at the Turning Five Review Meeting, be sure to prepare this person. Everyone on your team must be chanting the same tune when it comes to discussing what your child needs. You do not want any curve balls at this meeting! For example, if you want an ICT class in your local public school the last thing you want is for your child's SEIT to say that they think he needs to be in a District 75 program. Other professionals who know your child can also be asked to attend, but make sure that every person who does attend, whether in person or by telephone, is on the same page regarding the needs of your child.*

TIP

My strong advice is that at least one parent attend the CSE meeting in person and not by telephone. I cannot over-emphasize the importance of personally attending this meeting. If there are two parents, then I strongly recommend that both parents attend or that in lieu of both parents attending you bring a close friend or relative. It is important that someone take detailed notes. Four ears are better than two!

TIP

There is an optional member on the CSE review team known as the "Physician Member." This person is a medical doctor employed by the DOE. At a parent's request, made in writing 72 hours prior to the CSE review meeting, this person can be asked to attend a CSE review meeting to serve as a consultant/advisor. Once this person attends the review meeting he/she becomes a mandatory member. There are instances where I recommend the presence of the physician member, however, this determination is made on a case-by-case basis.

Should a Parent Bring an Attorney to the Turning Five Review Meeting?

The answer to this question must be made on a case-by-case basis. Different law firms and attorneys have different practices. In my firm, we send an attorney (or experienced advocate employed by our firm) to a CSE review meeting if the child has been accepted at an *approved* private special education school or if the parent is seeking a public school program that requires an extraordinary level of service.

There might be other instances where it is advisable that a parent have an attorney or advocate at a CSE review. For example, if a parent feels completely overwhelmed, or is otherwise not able to effectively communicate or advocate for their child, then a professional should be with them.

Similarly, there are instances when it is not advisable to have an attorney accompany a parent to the Turning Five Review Meeting. For example, if your child will be attending an independent private school, or if you are seeking another year of preschool services under an order of pendency, having an attorney will not be helpful at this meeting.

TIP

Regardless of whether an attorney is going with you to the CSE review or if you are attending on your own, you should always be thoroughly prepared for this meeting.

Purpose of the Turning Five Review Meeting

The New York State Education Department publishes a document that provides guidance to CSE/IEP review teams on the order of steps to be used in developing an IEP. They are as follows:

Step One: Obtain and consider evaluation material.

Step Two: Determine eligibility for special education services.

Step Three: Identify the student's present levels of performance and indicate the individual needs of the student in the areas of academic achievement, functional performance and learning characteristics, social development, physical development, and management needs.

Step Four: Identify the measurable postsecondary goals and transition needs, including courses of study of the student (this applies only to students age 15 and over).

Step Five: Set realistic and measurable annual goals for the student.

Step Six: Report progress to parents.

Step Seven: Determine the special education program and services the student will need.

I prefer to conceptualize the Turning Five Review as having a threefold purpose, which incorporates all of the DOE's seven steps:

(1) Eligibility and Classification;

(2) Development of an IEP;

(3) Program Recommendation.

What Will Happen at the Turning Five Review Meeting?

STEP ONE: Eligibility and Classification

The threshold question of eligibility is addressed at the onset of the Turning Five Review Meeting. The fact that a child has a preschool IEP does not automatically mean that the child will be eligible for an IEP and services through the school-age CSE. Eligibility criteria for CPSE is different than that of the school-age CSE. For CPSE, a child is determined to be eligible when they present with either a 12-month delay in one or more functional area(s); or a 33 percent delay in one functional area; or a 25 percent delay in each of two functional areas. When a child meets any of these formulaic criteria, they are given the generic classification of a "preschooler with a disability"; an IEP is developed and services are then provided.

For CSE students (turning five through 21) there is no objective formulaic standard used to determine whether a child is eligible for an IEP and educational placement and/or related services. For this group of students to be eligible for special education and related services through the CSE, they must meet the criteria for one of the thirteen educational "handicapping conditions" (classifications); and the disability must

The Big Event: Your Turning 5 Review

INVITATION OR TICKET

Date, time, place of meeting sent to parents

WHO IS THERE WITH YOU

Membership of the Review Team

- Parents
- School Psychologist
- District Representative
- General Education Teacher
- Special Education Teacher
- Optional (parent member, physician, others)

WHAT WILL HAPPEN AT THE MEETING

1. Determine if the child is eligible and meets criteria for classification.

2. Develop an Individualized Education Program (IEP).

   Description of child's educational needs.

   Goals created and reviewed with parents.

   Specific related services recommended.

3. Program Recommended

   Three considerations:

   Least Restrictive Environment (LRE).

   Phase 2 of the New Initiative.

   NYS Continuum (aka the menu of what the DOE has to offer).

impact on the child's school performance; *and* it must also require special education and/or related services. This determination is based upon the evaluations and reports that the CSE has available to them at the review meeting. The school-age CSE's determination of eligibility and classification is far more subjective, and is made by the members of the review team.

TIP

School performance is not limited solely to academics. Your child might be advanced academically yet have severe sensory issues, difficulty with attention, or social functioning problems. If these issues impact or will impact on classroom functioning this must be documented in the evaluations that you have submitted to the CSE review team. Be sure to raise this and discuss these issues with the team.

The 13 Classifications Recognized by New York State:

Autism: A developmental disability significantly affecting verbal and nonverbal communication and social interaction, generally evident before age 3.

Deaf Blindness: A simultaneous significant hearing loss and significant vision loss.

Deafness: A hearing impairment that is so severe that the student is impaired in processing linguistic information through hearing with or without amplification.

Emotional Disturbance: Significant problems in the social-emotional area over a long period of time to a degree that learning is negatively affected.

Hearing Impairment: A partial or complete loss of hearing.

Intellectual Disability: Significant limitations in intellectual ability and adaptive behavior. (This classification replaced mental retardation.)

Learning Disability: A disorder related to processing information that leads to difficulties in listening, thinking, reading, writing, and/or mathematical computing.

Multiple Disabilities: The simultaneous presence of two or more disabilities such that the child has severe educational needs that cannot be met by a program for one of the impairments.

Orthopedic Impairment: A significant physical limitation that impairs the ability to move or complete motor activities.

Other Health Impairment: A disease or health disorder so significant that it negatively affects learning. A child with a diagnosis of ADHD is often classified as having OHI.

Speech or Language Impairment: A disorder related to accurately producing the sounds of language or meaningfully using language to communicate.

Traumatic Brain Injury: An acquired injury to the brain with resulting impairments that adversely affect educational performance.

Visual Impairment, including Blindness: A partial or complete loss of vision.

These classifications should not be arbitrarily or carelessly assigned. A classification is very important, particularly if a parent is seeking admission to an approved private special education schools. Approved private special education schools are licensed for specific classifications. There is a significant difference between a diagnosis and a classification. A diagnosis is made by a pediatrician, neurologist, psychiatrist, or psychologist; whereas a classification for purposes of the CSE is made by the multidisciplinary review team. Classifications sometimes are also referred to as "educational handicapping conditions."

Questions about a child's specific diagnosis and what classification would best suit the child frequently arise. One potential problem is with the diagnosis of Asperger Syndrome (AS). In May 2013, the American Psychiatric Association published a new Diagnostic Statistical Manual (DSM-V). This manual eliminated Asperger Syndrome as a separate disorder and instead includes it under the diagnosis of Autism Spectrum Disorder (ASD). Understandably, many parents were upset with this change. The diagnosis of ASD presents a wide range of symptoms and functional abilities. For many children, simply categorizing them as ASD does not adequately portray their needs and issues, nor describe their strengths and abilities.

Similarly, a child who would have been given the diagnosis PDD-NOS prior to the change in the DSM may have met the criteria for Autism, Speech or Language Impairment, Other Health Impairment, Learning Disability, or Emotional Disturbance. However with the new DSM-V, school districts are more likely to classify the youngster with ASD.

You will note that there is no separate classification for a child with ADHD/ADD. Children with this diagnosis may be classified as Learning Disabled; Emotionally Disturbed, or Other Health Impaired.

If a child has a diagnosis but does not meet the eligibility criteria for classification, the child can still be eligible for services, accommodations, and modifications under Section 504 of the Rehabilitation Act of

1973. A 504 plan is made at a building or school level. It does not carry with it the same rights and privileges as an IEP, but it is an option for some children.

> TIP
>
> *In view of the fact that a 504 plan does not carry the same rights as an IEP, I generally prefer that a child be classified and an IEP be developed. Sometimes this will require strong advocacy.*

STEP TWO: Development of an IEP

What is an Individualized Education Program (IEP)?

An IEP is the written document produced at a CSE review. It is the cornerstone of a child's special education program. Once found eligible for special education and related services, the IEP must individually reflect the unique educational needs of the child. The IEP is intended to help a child reach his or her goals by guiding teachers and related service providers (including paraprofessionals) in understanding the child's disability and how it affects their learning processes.

The IEP must describe how the child learns, how he or she best demonstrates that learning, and what teachers and related service providers can and will do to help the child learn more effectively. As long as the child qualifies for special education, the IEP must be regularly reviewed and updated.

As of 2011, NYC uses an IEP format that is generated by a computer program known as SESIS. This program is cumbersome, completely computer driven, and not user friendly. Notwithstanding the limitations of SESIS, it has the ability to produce an IEP that complies with federal and state law. It is during this drafting phase of the IEP process that the team will be determining the academic and related service goals for your child. With the SESIS system, the IEP is no longer hand-written. Instead, it is done on a computer by one of the DOE representatives while the other participants are talking. A member of the CSE team should go over each and every goal with the parents and whoever else is participating on behalf of the student in order to get input as to the appropriateness and relevance of the goals.

> TIP
>
> *It is not your job to tell the review team what they are legally required to do; they should know this for themselves. Just keep notes!*

What are IEP goals?

IEP goals represent what a parent and other members of the IEP team think the child will be able to accomplish in one year's time in terms of academic, developmental, functional, social, emotional, physical, and management needs. Annual goals must be written in measurable terms, based on the child's present level of performance. Goals must relate to the areas of need identified in the section of the IEP called "present level of performance." For each annual goal, the IEP must indicate the evaluative criteria, which is the measure used to determine if the goal has been achieved; the evaluation procedures, which is how progress will be measured; and schedules of exactly when progress will be measured.

STEP THREE: Making a Program Recommendation

Once the threshold question of eligibility is satisfied and the review team has determined a classification and created the goals and objectives, they will turn to the critical question that is most important to parents: "What program will be recommended for the child?"

> TIP
> _____
>
> *Although you will be rushing to get to the question of program recommendation at the Turning Five Review Meeting you must allow the team to go through the entire process. Take detailed notes along the way and be patient. You will not leave the meeting without a program recommendation.*

In making a program recommendation, the CSE is bound by what I view as three considerations. The first consideration is something known as the **Least Restrictive Environment** (also referred to as "LRE"). The principle of LRE is found throughout special education law. The Individual with Disabilities Education Improvement Act, commonly known as the IDEA (the federal statute upon which all of special education law is based) requires that every student with a disability be educated in the "least restrictive environment" in which he or she can make meaningful educational progress. This means that, to the greatest extent possible, students with disabilities should be placed in general education classrooms alongside their non-disabled peers. Volumes have been written about this concept and it is referred to in almost every Impartial Hearing and court case concerning special education. It is particularly relevant for parents who are seeking either placement at, or reimbursement for, a private special education school. If you want to read more about the concept of LRE go to: *www.lrecoalition.org*. Parents who are seeking an inclusion program rely strongly on this concept and should have a full understanding of it.

The second consideration in the formulation of a program recommendation is embodied in something that the DOE refers to as "Phase Two of the New Initiative on Special Education." This initiative went into full effect in September 2012, expressing the DOE's policy that every local home-zoned public school should be able to meet the IEP needs of every child. This initiative is inconsistently applied amongst the ten regions. There are review teams that refuse to even consider a deferral to the Central Based Support Team (CBST) for private school, informing parents that the CSE in that region is prohibited from doing so, while there are other regions and teams that, even when not expected, make a recommendation for private school placement.

> TIP
> _An "initiative" is not a law; it is a written but somewhat unofficial policy, describing an action or behavior that will be followed._

The third consideration and the one that is most important for parents, is something known as New York City's **Continuum of Special Education Programs**. We refer to this as "the continuum," which requires that school districts have available to all classified students a _continuum_ of services and programs that can be used to meet a child's individualized needs. I like to refer to this as a school district's "menu." You will note that it starts with the least restrictive setting, and the least amount of services, and that it then goes up and the setting gets more restrictive each step of the way.

The New York City Continuum of Special Education Programs

General Education with Related Services

This means that a child is referred to a general education class in a public school (with or without a paraprofessional) and is recommended to receive one or more of the following related services: Speech and Language Therapy; Occupational Therapy; Physical Therapy; Vision or Hearing Therapy. This is the least amount of services that can be offered with an IEP.

There are two types of paraprofessionals, commonly referred to as "paras": (1) a "health para," for children whose medical needs require the presence of an adult; and (2) a "behavior management para," for children whose behaviors interfere with their classroom functioning. With the onset of the DOE's 2012 "New Initiative," and its stated goal that all children be accommodated in a general education setting, review teams are recommending paraprofessionals with greater frequency.

The frequency and duration of the related services a child will receive as a school-age student will typically be less than what they received in their preschool program under the CPSE. This is true even if a parent submits documentation substantiating a need for the continuation of the preschool mandates.

TIP

This disparity between what the professionals who work with your child are recommending and what the review team is recommending can be used to prove that an IEP is not appropriate for a specific child.

General Education with Special Education Teacher Support Services (SETSS)

This program used to be called "resource room." In one of the many NYC reorganizations the name changed to SETSS. A student who is in either a general education or ICT class will be pulled out of class to meet with a special education teacher in a small group with other students. The group will work on areas that have been identified as troublesome for the child. Recently the DOE has recommended SETSS along with an ICT placement. Sometimes the SETSS teacher will come into the classroom to provide the service to the child. This is referred to as "push-in." When a child is taken out of the classroom for SETSS service this is referred to as "pull-out." The push-in or pull-out models are also used for providing related services.

Integrated Co-Teaching (ICT)

In an ICT (sometimes referred to as a CTT, or Collaborative Team Teaching) class up to 40% of the students have IEPs. The class has one special education teacher who co-teaches with a general education teacher in a general education class. The class size can range from twenty to thirty or more students. A placement recommendation in an ICT class is considered to be a placement within a general education setting and follows a standard grade-level curriculum.

TIP

The ICT model is a good one, but the problem is that the class size is often far too large. There are some very good ICT classes in select public schools; however, parents do not have the option to pick and choose the school they want.

TIP

Some schools only offer ICT on a part-time basis. If this is a program that you want for your child, ask the team at the meeting if the recommendation will be a full-time or part-time ICT program.

The ASD NEST Program

This is one of the most coveted public school special education programs that NYC offers. It is a small inclusion class for high-functioning children who have an autism spectrum diagnosis. This small inclusion class has a total of twelve general and special education children. Generally, there are four special needs children and eight general education children. All of the special education students are classified as having autism. Admission to the NEST program is determined solely by the staff running the program. The admission process is difficult and there are always far more applicants than available seats.

TIP

For many students, the NEST Program is as good as it gets in terms of the NYC public schools. I strongly encourage all clients, whose children meet the profile for admission to this program, to explore it as an option. Start early and develop a relationship with the NEST coordinator in your district/region. I have often seen that the parents who vigorously and actively pursue NEST have a better chance of at least getting their child considered for this program.

Intensive Kindergarten is a 6:1:1 class for children who could meet the eligibility for NEST placement but need another year of intensive services in the areas of social and language development as well as behavioral support. This is also a highly coveted program for a child with an ASD diagnosis since it often leads to admission to NEST kindergarten the following year.

TIP

There is also a general education NEST program for children who test in the gifted and talented range. Do not confuse these programs, they are very different.

Special Class in a Community School

This refers to a small class with a student-to-teacher ratio of either 12:1 or 12:1:1 (for elementary and middle schools) and 15:1 (for high school). These are small, self-contained classes within local public schools. They vary from school to school in terms of the quality of the program and the type of student served. In theory, these classes are supposed to be homogeneous, meaning students are supposed to be placed in "suitable and functional groups for instructional purposes."

TIP

Unfortunately, most self-contained classes are not homogeneous and there is a wide range of functioning of students in these classes. If this is a program that you are considering, try and observe the

*class and speak with the teacher before you agree to it. Describe
your child to the teacher or supervisor of special education at the
public school. If you have a private evaluation, share it with school
faculty and make sure that this is what you want for your child.*

Special Class in a Specialized School

In New York City, this is known as **District 75**. The majority of
District 75 programs serve children on the autism spectrum. However,
they also serve children with severe physical needs and/or emotionally
disturbed students. The class sizes of District 75 programs are: 6:1:1, 8:1:1,
or 12:1:4, and a few 12:1:1. These are always 12-month programs.

Defer to CBST for Non-Public NYS-Approved Private School Placement
(See Chapter Three)

Home or Hospital-Based Instruction

This program is for children who are too ill to go to a school site.
The DOE will send a teacher to the home or hospital. It is supposed to
be an interim program and should not be confused with home schooling,
where parents opt out of public education.

TIP

*Parents often confuse home instruction with home schooling. They
are not the same. If either is an option that you are considering, be
sure you understand the difference and the legal ramifications.*

The Conclusion of the Turning Five Review Meeting

The Turning Five Review Meeting generally lasts between forty-
five minutes to an hour and a quarter. Of course there are instances
where a meeting can last several hours or only a few minutes, but these
are the rare exceptions. During the spring, which is the busiest time of
year, the review teams usually schedule several meetings a day and are
very conscious of keeping to their schedule. After the program recommendation is made, in most instances, the person leading the meeting
will announce that the meeting is over. Generally parents are not given
an IEP at the conclusion of the meeting, but are told that one will be
mailed to them, along with a specific placement recommendation.

There is a subtle but important distinction between a "program"
and a "specific placement." The generic type of program should be
discussed and recommended at the Turning Five Review Meeting. The
actual placement is sent to the parents by mail weeks or months after
the meeting.

What if a parent disagrees with the proposed program recommendation?

It is not at all unusual for parents to disagree with the generic recommendation being made for their child by the review team. The following tips should help in dealing with a situation where a parent finds themselves disagreeing with a program recommendation made by the turning-five team.

TIP
_____

Clearly and openly state that you disagree with the program recommendation. Indicate specifically what it is about the recommended program that you disagree with. Is the class size too large? Is the school building too loud and chaotic? Is the environment in the school potentially dangerous for your child? If you observed the lunchroom or school yard, is there something in these settings that is not appropriate for your child? If so, tell the team what your concerns are.

TIP
_____

After you state your disagreements you must always follow it up with a statement that although you disagree, you are willing to keep an open mind and will visit and consider whatever the CSE recommends. Then add something to the effect that you hope that the CSE will similarly keep an open mind if you were to reject the placement and that they will be amenable to further discussions.

TIP
_____

If you have already visited the type of program that the team is recommending and you believe it is not appropriate for your child, tell this to the team. Be specific and detailed about your visit(s). Indicate the date(s) you went, what you saw and why you believe this would not work. But again always indicate your willingness to revisit with an open mind.

TIP
_____

If the team recommends a self-contained class, ask them if all classes are the same or is there a difference in the student population between classes.

TIP
_____

Whatever you do, no matter how angry or upset you may become, do not get into an argument or screaming match with the review team. A parent should always be cooperative and courteous and in

New York State Continuum of Special Education Programs

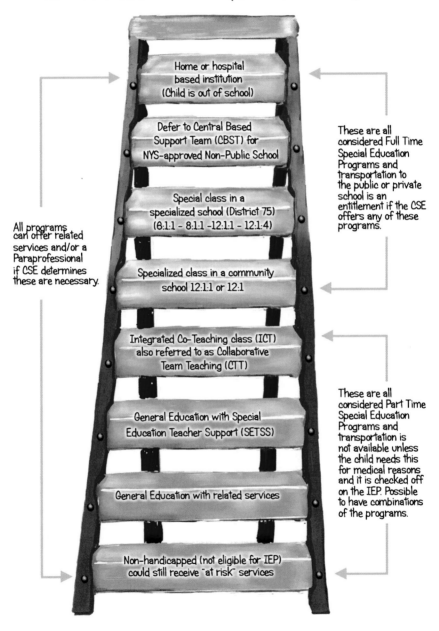

no way disrupt the process. But, hold firm to your beliefs. Keep repeating in your mind the mantra, "Kind, but firm."

TIP

As soon as you leave the meeting, while things are fresh in your memory, make a detailed journal entry as to what occurred, who said what, and the outcome of all discussions.

TIP

If you believe you were treated poorly at the Turning Five Review Meeting, write to the chairperson indicating your disagreement with what occurred at the review meeting. However, if you are using an attorney or advocate, check with them first.

Final Notice of Recommendation

Sometime after the Turning Five Review Meeting, and generally before June 15th, parents will be mailed a written form called a *Final Notice of Recommendation (FNR)*. This form letter places the child in a specific school and a specific class. Although this notice sometimes indicates that a parent must respond within ten days of receipt, the date of response is not a legal requirement. This is simply the DOE's request in order to plan their classes accordingly. The placement indicated in the final notice is the DOE's official turning-five recommendation. This would be the actual recommendation that would be challenged in an Impartial Hearing request.

TIP

I recommend that parents respond to the final notice in a timely manner. But, before responding, I recommend that a parent visit the proposed program. For me, the actual school visit is critical, even if you have already visited a similar program, or even the same program before it was officially recommended.

TIP

Sometimes I recommend hiring and taking an "expert" with you on the official school visit. The official visit is the one made after the DOE issues their final notice. This expert can be your child's SEIT, a related service provider, or a private consultant.

TIP

After your visit to the recommended placement, if you determine that it is not appropriate for your child, but you still want a public school placement, you can try to get an alternate public school

placement. This is very difficult; sometimes almost as difficult as getting a private school settlement. You can ask for a meeting with the district's placement officer or even go to mediation.

TIP

If after visiting the recommended public school you find it inappropriate and you intend on sending your child to a private special education school, contact your attorney for specific advice as to how to respond to the final notice.

TIP

Although the final notice indicates that if you disagree with the recommendation you should file for an Impartial Hearing, do not do this if you are being represented by an attorney. Filing for an Impartial Hearing is your attorney's job! The current statute of limitations gives parents up to two years from their IEP meeting to file for a hearing, not ten days from the notice.

What if a child is not vaccinated or does not have current vaccinations?

There are some parents who have not vaccinated their turning-five child, or their child has not completed the full complement of required vaccinations. New York State requires that all children be fully vaccinated in order to attend a public school. Many preschools do not have this requirement and are much more lenient in granting an exemption to this requirement. There are some private schools that require vaccinations and others that will grant their own exemptions to this requirement. Over the years there are far fewer private schools that grant exemptions.

For public schools, the only exemptions to the vaccination require-ment are based on either a bona fide religious belief or very specific health/medical issues. In order to receive an exemption from vaccina-tions, you must file a formal request with the Department of Health and Mental Hygiene. Go to *http://schools.nyc.gov/Offices/Health/ImmunizationInfo/ default.htm* and follow the instructions. If you are rejected, there is an appeal process.

TIP

If you are not going to vaccinate your child and you have not been granted a medical exemption, you should inform the review team of this fact sometime during the Turning Five Review Meeting and ask what your options are.

CHAPTER THREE

Special Education Private Schools

New York City is the capital of private special education schools. Families come from all over the world to take advantage of the high quality special education schools and services available to children with special needs. The list of private schools found in this chapter confirms this wealth of opportunity. Each private school caters to a specific type of child and provides a highly specialized program and services. Even with tight budgets, new private schools and programs open each year and fill their seats with little difficulty. Existing schools are expanding and waiting lists, even with an early application, are not uncommon.

This chapter will provide an overview of the types of private special education schools, tips on how to maximize a child's chance of admission, and how a parent can be in the best possible position to receive either direct funding or tuition reimbursement.

> TIP
>
> *If you are planning on applying to private special education schools with the hopes of having this placement directly funded or reimbursed by the DOE, meet with an attorney who specializes in this type of law and who has experience in suing for funding and reimbursement. I recommend doing this at the beginning of your child's last year of preschool.*

Parents often use the term funding and tuition reimbursement interchangeably. This is a common misnomer.

The term "funding" technically means that the DOE directly pays an approved private school for the tuition of a child placed at that school by the Central Based Support team (CBST). This requires a CSE review team to recommend that the child's care be deferred to CBST for NYS Approved Non-Public School.

The term "tuition reimbursement" means a parent pays the private school in advance of the child actually attending, or while the child is attending, and then sues the DOE for reimbursement of the tuition already paid. Often the term "funding" is used to apply to both situations, but they are technically different.

Two Categories of Special Education Private Schools

In New York State there are two categories of private special education schools: **Approved** and **Independent**. From an educational and clinical perspective, there is little difference between these two categories. There are nuanced differences between specific schools and the populations served at each school can vary. A private special education school should maximize the chances of a child becoming the best student that he or she can be.

TIP

You know your child best and must use your own eyes and ears to determine whether a school is right. There is something that I refer to as "school karma." It's either there or it's not. Finding a school is no different than buying a home. When looking for a home most of us can tell on the first visit whether we could see ourselves living there.

TIP

When you visit a school, ask yourself the threshold question of whether you could see your child in this program. Watch the children that are attending, watch the staff interacting with them, and meet with the administrators. Your subjective opinion is very important.

TIP

Try and speak with parents whose children attend the school you are considering. Either ask the school for a list of parent references or go into any of the internet special needs chat rooms. There will always be the occasional parent who is not happy with a school, but consider the majority opinion about any school you are applying to.

TIP

Evaluators, educational consultants, lawyers, and most NYC advocates are familiar with approved and independent schools. These professionals can help you narrow your choices.

Similarities Between Approved and Independent Schools

1. High quality of education

These schools provide a high quality of education with individualized attention and instruction. Communication between parents and school personnel is a key ingredient to the success and popularity of these schools.

2. Admission procedures

It is at the complete discretion of the private school who they accept or reject. Usually there is an admissions committee that makes

Two Categories of Private Special Education Schools

SIMILARITIES

Approved & Independent

- Provide high quality of education.
- Good communication between school and parents.
- Complete discretion of the school as to who they accept or reject.
- Detailed application and admission procedures.
- Some schools accept private pay as well as funded students.
- Majority have non-profit status.
- Have specific areas of expertise.

DIFFERENCES

Approved

- There is a mechanism (a chance) of having the CSE recommend and directly fund placement at an approved school by choosing "Defer to CBST" option on the continuum. If this happens no need for a lawyer every year. Your case is done!

- Generally case "reapps" (gets re-approval) every after the first year.

- If DOE refuses to defer to CBST parent can pay privately and sue.

- Nickerson Letter can apply.

- Does not have to accept private pay, at a school's discretion.

- Has to adhere to NYS standards and subject to audits by NYS and NYC.

- Licensed for specific classifications, and can only be funded for students having an IEP with these classifications.

- Follows a DOE calendar.

Independent

- No mechanism for CSE to recommend and directly fund.

- Parents must pay in full and sue every year.

- Need lawyer every year to sue.

- Rates set by their own board and generally increase each year.

- Not bound by CSE classifications.

- No need for an IEP or DOE involvement if the parent does not intend to seek reimbursement from DOE.

- Does not follow a DOE calendar.

this determination. There are detailed applications and rigorous admission procedures involved before an acceptance or rejection is issued. Some schools have rolling admissions, meaning that applications may be submitted throughout the year and the school will either accept or reject the child as soon as the application is reviewed, while other schools have a firm deadline and will wait to get all the applications in before they choose from the pool of applicants.

> ### TIP
> *Be certain to find out the deadline for submitting an application to a specific school and adhere to it. If a school has rolling admissions, get your application in early.*

> ### TIP
> *If you are applying to multiple schools, which most parents do, create a grid or chart for yourself so that you do not confuse the schools.*

3. A current and comprehensive evaluation needed

These schools generally require an evaluation that was done within the past year. The evaluation must include a social, developmental and family history, observations of the child, a measure of the child's intelligence, and an academic assessment. Some schools request a language evaluation while others require personality assessments.

> ### TIP
> *Because an evaluation is such an important part of the admission and funding process I generally recommend having this done privately. (See Chapter Six)*

4. Open houses, tours, and websites

All established private special education schools in NYC have websites. Keep in mind that these are promotional in nature and do not always answer specific questions. In addition to websites and printed materials, most of these schools have open houses or tours. There are some schools that require a parent to apply for admission before allowing a visit. These schools will invite the child and parent to tour only after the application is submitted and the director of admissions has determined suitability.

> ### TIP
> *I strongly recommend visiting as many schools as possible and keeping a log/journal of your visit and impressions; you should become a highly educated consumer.*

TIP

If you cannot get a tour of a school, or you have to wait weeks for an opening on a tour, stop by the school to pick up the application. You can also go to the school and watch the children arriving in the morning or leaving in the afternoon. How a school handles arrival and dismissal is very telling. You will also get an opportunity to take a look at the children attending the school and the level of supervision and attention that they are receiving. (I pass a private school on my way to work every morning and am impressed by how the staff greets and supervises the students as they arrive.)

5. **Acceptance at the school does not mean that the CSE thinks, agrees, or believes that the child needs placement at a private school**

Some parents have the misconception that because their child was accepted at an approved or independent school that this is proof positive to the CSE that the child needs this school placement. Unfortunately, this is not the case. A child's acceptance at a school does not create a mandate for the child to attend that school at the district's expense. Parents want what is best for their child. However, legally all that a school district has to provide is a placement that is "merely appropriate." What this means is that the DOE does not have to provide a child with the best possible school placement. The DOE's obligation is met by offering a program that is "merely appropriate." In the case of an approved school, what the acceptance does mean for the parent is that there is a chance that the CSE *might* recommend and fund the placement.

6. **Expensive**

Approved and independent private special education schools in NYC are expensive. The per capita cost of educating a child in a private special education school is far more than the cost of educating that same child in a NYC public school.

Differences Between Approved and Independent Schools

1. Funding

The critical difference between an approved and independent school relates to who pays for the school and how payment happens. As previously mentioned the term "funding" is different from "reimbursement."

Funding technically refers to when a school district pays the school directly for the placement of a specific child. *Reimbursement* happens when the school district pays the parent, either fully or partially, for the tuition that the parent has already paid.

Funding for an Approved School Placement

There are three ways that a parent can be funded when they place their child at an approved school:

"Defer to CBST for a NYS Approved Non-Public School"

Placement of a child at an approved private special education school is an option on the NYC Continuum of Programs. In other words, it's on the menu—not often served, but still part of the menu. The CSE review team must make this recommendation.

To get a CSE review team to make this recommendation, they must be convinced that the child's unusual and unique needs cannot be met in any of the public school programs that also appear on the NYC continuum. I call this the "bucket approach," meaning that the child doesn't fit into the existing buckets that the DOE has to offer.

> TIP
> _____
>
> *The documentation available to the review team at the time of the meeting is critical. In order to convince the CSE review team to defer your child's case to the CBST, make sure all of your reports, evaluations, and experts are making this recommendation and providing sufficient justification.*

> TIP
> _____
>
> *It is not sufficient for an evaluation or a therapist's report to simply give a conclusion, i.e. "the child needs a private school." Throughout the entire body of the independent evaluation and report there needs to be strong support for this recommendation. For example, a child with ADHD cannot sufficiently focus in a large classroom.*

Although the review team cannot recommend a specific school, they can recommend the generic category of "Defer to CBST for NYS Approved Non-Public School." Once the CSE agrees to this deferral, they then prepare the file, which they now refer to as the "packet," and send it to the CBST office. Before going to the CBST, a senior clinician at the CSE will review the file. This packet must contain a specific rationale detailing why the child's needs cannot be met in a public school program. It must also contain a current psycho-educational evaluation, a physical examination, and other supporting clinical documentation.

> TIP
> _____
>
> *Since the review team needs a very strong justification or rationale for this recommendation, I suggest you have your notes ready for*

Funding Path For Private Special Education Schools

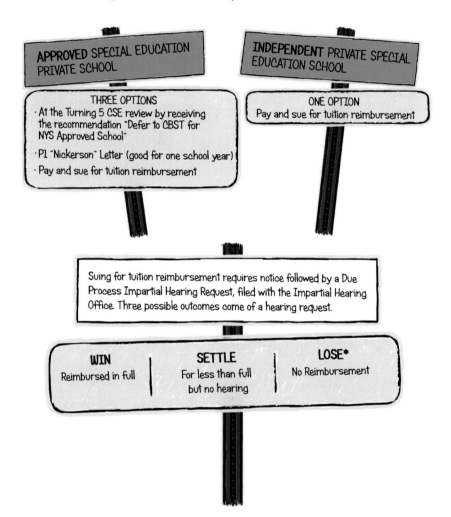

APPROVED SPECIAL EDUCATION PRIVATE SCHOOL

THREE OPTIONS
- At the Turning 5 CSE review by receiving the recommendation "Defer to CBST for NYS Approved School"
- P1 "Nickerson" Letter (good for one school year)
- Pay and sue for tuition reimbursement

INDEPENDENT PRIVATE SPECIAL EDUCATION SCHOOL

ONE OPTION
Pay and sue for tuition reimbursement

Suing for tuition reimbursement requires notice followed by a Due Process Impartial Hearing Request, filed with the Impartial Hearing Office. Three possible outcomes come of a hearing request.

WIN
Reimbursed in full

SETTLE
For less than full but no hearing

LOSE*
No Reimbursement

*Whoever is the losing party at an Impartial Hearing has an automatic right of appeal. All appeals of an Impartial Hearing must first go to the NYS Department of Education Office of State Review (SRO). **Dangerous territory!**

*the team so that you can actually assist in the process. Do not give
the team your notes; just reference them throughout your discussion.*

TIP

*Be sure that the acceptance letter sent to you by the approved school
is part of the packet being sent to CBST. This will assist the CBST
representative. (Remember to do this only if for an approved school.)*

Once the case arrives at CBST, it is assigned to a case manager who
reviews the file. If the child has been accepted at an approved school, the
case manager contacts the approved school to confirm the acceptance
and to send over forms for funding.

TIP

*The best advice (and it's worth repeating) is to have strong
arguments and specific reasons as to why the public school options
are not appropriate.*

TIP

*Outside of New York City (Long Island, Westchester, and other
counties) there is no CBST office. School districts can refer
students and fund them at the approved schools if they are similarly convinced that there are no public school programs. Outside
of NYC, this is referred to as an "out-of-district placement."*

Issuance of a P-1 Nickerson Letter

The second way of receiving funding for placement at an approved
school is through the issuance of a *P-1 Nickerson Letter*. A Nickerson
Letter is the result of a 1979 federal class action lawsuit known as Jose P.
v. Mills. This lawsuit was brought by parent advocacy groups against
the New York City Board of Education (BOE) as a result of the failure of
the BOE to respond to referrals which resulted in enormous delays in
evaluating and offering placements to children with special needs.
Presiding over this lawsuit was the late and highly regarded Judge
Eugene Nickerson. Judge Nickerson directed the NYC Board of Education (BOE) to adhere to a time frame for evaluating a child, developing
an IEP, and issuing a placement. Here is some specific language from the
Nickerson stipulation:

*(1) for a child not known to the CSE or CPSE, within 60 schools days
of the referral to the CSE for either an evaluation or a review meeting;
(2) if the child is known to the CSE by virtue of being a CPSE student,
a CSE must hold a review, develop an IEP and issue a specific placement recommendation on or before June 15th of the year preceding the*

child's required entrance to kindergarten. (For school-aged children the date becomes August 15th.)

If the BOE (now DOE) fails to adhere to these time frames, the school district is required to issue a voucher-like form called a P-1 letter. This letter is what is commonly referred to as a Nickerson Letter. *The P-1/Nickerson Letter grants funding for a child for one academic year, but only at an approved school, and only under very specific circumstances.*

The P-1/Nickerson Letter is different from having a CSE review team defer a child's case to CBST. A Nickerson Letter is a remedy available only when the DOE fails to offer a child a public school program/placement by a set date. It is not a determination by a CSE review team that a child's needs cannot be met in a public school program. As such, it should always be a fall-back position if a team refuses a deferral.

There are significant limitations to a Nickerson Letter. First, there is an expiration date on the P-1 form. This date means that if a parent does not secure a seat for their child in an approved school by the expiration date on this form, it is no longer valid.

> **TIP**
>
> *If you have already secured a seat for your child in one of the approved schools and you are issued a P-1 "Nickerson" Letter, immediately bring the letter to the approved school and they will complete and submit back to the district a P-2 form, whereby the school is accepting your child under the contract terms they have with the DOE.*

> **TIP**
>
> *There are a few approved schools that do not accept Nickerson Letters. This has to do with the arrangement that they have made with the DOE. Ask the approved school that you are applying to if they accept Nickerson Letters.*

Another limitation to a Nickerson Letter is that the funding is only valid for one year. Many times a child will be funded for their first year at an approved school through a Nickerson Letter, and for subsequent years their case is deferred to the CBST. However, this is not a guarantee of future approval, and the CSE may refuse to defer the case to CBST in subsequent years.

From my perspective, the most critical limitation of a Nickerson Letter, is that it can only be used when the underlying recommendation by the team is for a full-time special education class. Let me give you an example, so you fully understand this limitation:

Understanding the Nickerson Letter (P1) for a Turning 5 Student

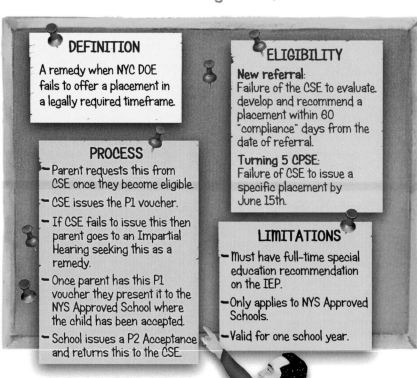

DEFINITION

A remedy when NYC DOE fails to offer a placement in a legally required timeframe.

ELIGIBILITY

New referral:
Failure of the CSE to evaluate. develop and recommend a placement within 60 "compliance" days from the date of referral.

Turning 5 CPSE:
Failure of CSE to issue a specific placement by June 15th.

PROCESS

- Parent requests this from CSE once they become eligible.
- CSE issues the P1 voucher.
- If CSE fails to issue this then parent goes to an Impartial Hearing seeking this as a remedy.
- Once parent has this P1 voucher they present it to the NYS Approved School where the child has been accepted.
- School issues a P2 Acceptance and returns this to the CSE.

LIMITATIONS

- Must have full-time special education recommendation on the IEP.
- Only applies to NYS Approved Schools.
- Valid for one school year.

Molly had her Turning Five Review Meeting at the end of April 2016. Her parents submitted a detailed neuropsychological evaluation to the CSE establishing that she is an extremely bright little girl, but nonetheless has significant language and fine motor delays. Molly was offered a spot at the Churchill School for September 2016. Her parents strongly believed that she would not be able to learn in an Integrated Co-Teaching (ICT) program and that she was far too intelligent for the 12:1:1 class. The parent used an attorney who accompanied her to CSE review meeting. Upon entering the meeting, it was obvious to the parent and the attorney that the CSE review team had read the private evaluation. Within two minutes the CSE classified Molly as speech and language impaired. However, when it came time to make a program recommendation, the team began by telling the parent that they were going to recommend an ICT class for Molly due to her high cognitive abilities. Molly's parent and her attorney respectfully disagreed with this recommendation asking for a deferral to CBST for a nonpublic school. The parent and attorney went over why every option, other than deferral, was not appropriate for Molly. As hard as they tried, and after an hour of intense discussion, the review team would only recommended a small 12:1 class in a community school. The attorney told the parent that this was not a perfect outcome but much better than ICT, and they accepted this conditioned upon the suitability of the specific class.

The person from the district in charge of the review team acknowledged that there were many self-contained classes in the district and the placement officer from the district would be responsible for sending notice to the parent of the specific class that Molly would be referred to. The parent was also told that they would receive Molly's IEP in the mail. Well, it was well after June 16th and nothing had arrived from the DOE indicating the final placement. BINGO! Molly is Nickerson-eligible. The attorney immediately filed for an Impartial Hearing seeking the issuance of a P-1 Nickerson Letter as a remedy. The district agreed, knowing that they had failed to adhere to the required deadlines. Before Molly even started at Churchill, her funding and busing were all worked out as a result of the P1 Nickerson Letter. They understood that the funding was only for one school year. Had Molly been given an IEP with an ICT recommendation the Nickerson Letter would not have been issued nor have been an available remedy for an untimely placement.

TIP

Recently, the DOE has stopped issuing Nickerson Letters even when we believe a parent is eligible for one. The DOE's claim is that a hearing officer has no right to order a Nickerson (P-1) Letter. The battles are ongoing. I recommend that parents not solely rely on the belief that they will receive a Nickerson (P-1)

*Letter. A parent must have backup funds available to pay tuition
and sue for reimbursement.*

Tuition reimbursement

The third way in which parents can attempt to receive "funding"
for the placement of their child at an approved special education private
school is by suing for tuition reimbursement for the fees they paid to the
private school. (This is the only option available for children who attend
independent schools.)

There are a small number of approved schools that do not accept
private pay students. This has to do with an agreement that the specific
school has with New York State Education Department. You must ask this
question when you apply. If your first choice school is one that does not
accept private pay students then you must have a backup "safety" school.

TIP

*A parent can file for and represent themselves at an Impartial
Hearing. When a parent does this they are known as a pro-se
litigant. I strongly discourage this course of action, particularly in
lawsuits involving tuition reimbursement where the stakes are
high. (See Chapter Five, Impartial Hearings, for a detailed
understanding of this process.)*

TIP

*There are many families that borrow money from relatives in
order to pay the tuition at private special education schools. This
is perfectly reasonable; however, the law calls for reimbursement
to the parents, not to grandparents or other relatives. If you are in
this situation, I recommend that before making any payments, you
immediately confer with your attorney/advocate as to how this
can be handled.*

Funding for an Independent School

As you can see from the chart on page 71, suing for tuition reimbursement is the only option available for a parent whose child attends
an independent school, as compared to being one of three options for a
child who attends an approved school.

When a parent sues for tuition reimbursement at an approved
school, they are doing this as a result of the United States Supreme
Court case known as "Burlington." When a parent sues for tuition
reimbursement at an independent school they are doing this as a result
of the Supreme Court case known as "Carter." In both situations, suing
for tuition reimbursement requires that a parent provide the school

district with a specific ten-day statutory notice, followed by the filing of a detailed due process Impartial Hearing request. This is sometimes referred to as "the complaint."

The judge at the Impartial Hearing is known as an impartial hearing officer (IHO). The IHO makes a determination as to whether to award the parent reimbursement by applying the Burlington/Carter three-prong test for tuition reimbursement. These three prongs are: (1) the school district failed to offer the child a Free Appropriate Public Education (FAPE); (2) the private school that the parent has chosen is reasonably calculated to confer a benefit to the child; and (3) the equities weigh in favor of the parent receiving an award of tuition reimbursement.

Differences Between Approved and Independent Schools (continued)

After understanding that the critical difference between approved and independent schools is the way in which the placement can be funded, I want readers to also understand some other important differences between these two categories of schools.

2. Setting of rates and costs

Approved schools have their tuition rates set by the New York State Education Department. These rates are fixed and are not reflective of the true cost of educating the student. The audits and paperwork required by the city and state for an approved school are overwhelming.

> **TIP**
>
> *Every approved school that I know operates with a significant per student deficit and relies heavily on donations and fundraising. Be prepared for this if your child attends such a school.*

Independent schools set their tuition rate on an annual basis and generally this is determined by the board of directors of that specific school. These rates are more reflective of the true cost of educating a child.

> **TIP**
>
> *If your child attends an independent school, be prepared to see an annual increase in the tuition, as well as pressure to participate in fundraising events.*

3. Classification requirement for funding at an approved school

A component of the agreement between an approved school and the New York State Education Department is that the approved school can only accept students with certain classifications. *This means for a child to have their approved school placement prospectively funded by the school district,* the child must have the specific classification for which the school is licensed. The classification requirement does not mean that the approved school cannot accept a child who has no classification or a classification that is different than the ones for which they are licensed. What it means is that the placement *cannot be prospectively funded* by the DOE until the classification conforms to the approved school's license. Let me give you an example:

When Billy was three years old, he was diagnosed by a developmental pediatrician with high-functioning PDD-NOS. At his Turning Five Review Meeting, his parents agreed to have him classified as having autism, so that he could be attend the ASD NEST program. Three years later, the NEST program was no longer meeting Billy's needs. At his annual meeting, the CSE review team agreed that he needed a private special education school for third grade, and they deferred his case to CBST. If Billy was going to attend a school like Learning Spring, which is licensed to serve children classified with autism, he'd be placed and funded without any difficulty. However, before the meeting, Billy's parents, on their own, applied to the Summit School, which accepted him. His parents wanted him to attend this school, however there is a problem. Summit School is not licensed for Autism; it is licensed only for the following classifications: Emotional Disturbance, Learning Disability, or Other Health Impairment. Summit accepts both private pay students as well as students deferred from CBST. Their admissions team is more concerned about whether a child fits into the school's profile and the specific class than the label or classification given by a CSE review team.

There is an answer to this potential problem, but it will require some work. In this instance, I would have Billy's parents get a current private evaluation. This evaluation would have to give strong and solid clinical support to justify a change in classification. In this fact pattern, the time to consult with an attorney would be when the parents knew that NEST was no longer working.

An independent school does not have a strict classification requirement. They assess the child based on their levels of performance and functioning as well as whether the child would fit into the school and the class; classification is secondary.

4. Permanency of placement

If the CSE agrees to place and fund a child at an approved school the case is over, and the parents no longer need the services of an attorney or advocate.

Generally in this situation, parents do not need to worry about the future funding of the child's placement. This means no more lawyers, no more lawsuits, no more expensive private evaluations, and no more sleepless nights. There are instances where several years after being placed at an approved school, the CSE determines that the child no longer needs this placement. This problem is surmountable. (See Chapter Four, Pendency)

In contrast, if a child attends an independent school, each and every year the parents must pay the tuition upfront and sue for reimbursement.

5. Calendar and curriculum

Approved schools follow the DOE calendar and New York State curriculum and graduation requirements. Whereas an independent school sets its own dates of operation and does not have to follow the state curriculum.

6. Related services

An approved school must follow the student's IEP and provide whatever related services appear on it. An independent school does not have to do this and can change the delivery of the related services to fit into their own program design. It is not bound by the IEP the way an approved school is.

7. Credentials

The teaching, administrative, and related service providers at an approved school must meet New York State requirements. All teachers must hold certification in special education. Administrators must be licensed, and related service providers must hold licenses and/or certification in their field. Independent schools are not bound by these requirements.

Lists of Approved and Independent Schools

The schools on these lists are not limited to turning-five students and many serve older students as well. *Because a school appears on these lists, it is by no means an endorsement or recommendation.* It simply means that during the course of my 40-year career in special education, I have heard of these schools and believe, for certain children, they are worth exploring. Here is the link for a complete list of the approved schools: *www.p12.nysed.gov/specialed/privateschools/853-statewide.htm.*

I have not listed or even discussed residential schools since only once in my career did I assist a parent with this type of placement for a turning-five child. You will note that some of the schools on this list are for older students. I have listed them in this publication because it is worth knowing what is available for future years.

Having approved status does not imply that a school is educationally or clinically better than an independent school. It simply means that decades ago the school made the decision to apply to the New York State Education Department Office of Special Education for designation as a New York State Approved School. Once approved by the State

Education Department, the school is on a list promulgated by the Commissioner of Education as being licensed to provide special education to a select population of students when the public schools cannot meet a child's needs.

Approved schools in and around New York City

AHRC - Brooklyn Blue Feather Elementary (Brooklyn)
AMAC - Association for Metroarea Autistic Children (Manhattan)
ANDRUS Children's Center - Orchard School (Yonkers)
Ascent (Deer Park)
Birch Family Services (Manhattan, Queens)
Bishop Ford High School (Brooklyn)
Block Institute (Brooklyn)
Blythedale Children's Hospital (Valhalla)
Catherine Laboure Special Education Program (Brooklyn)
Center for Developmental Disabilities (Woodbury)
Center for Discovery (Harris)
Community School (New Jersey)
The Child School (Roosevelt Island)
The Churchill School (Manhattan)
Cleary School for the Deaf (Nesconset)
Developmental Disabilities Institute (DDI) (Smithtown,
    Ronkonoma)
Eden II (Staten Island)
Eden II - Genesis School (Long Island)
Gillen Brewer (Manhattan)
Hagedorn Little Village School (Seaford)
The Hallen School (New Rochelle)
Harmony Heights School (Oyster Bay)
Hawthorne Country Day School (Manhattan, Hawthorne)
The HeartShare School (Brooklyn)
Hebrew Academy for Special Children (HASC) (Brooklyn,
    Long Island)
The Henry Viscardi School (Albertson)
Jewish Guild for the Blind - The Harriet and Robert Heilbrunn
    Guild School (Manhattan)
The Karafin School (Mt. Kisco)
Lavelle School for the Blind (Bronx)
League School (Brooklyn)
Learning Spring (Manhattan)
Lexington School for the Deaf (Queens)
Lifeline Center for Child Development (Queens)
Little Flower School (Wading River)

The Lorge School (Manhattan)
Lowell (Queens)
The Martin C. Barell School (Commack)
The Martin De Porres School (Brooklyn, Queens)
Mill Neck Manor School for the Deaf (Long Island)
The New LIFE School (Bronx)
NYC Autism Charter School - *Note: admission is solely by lottery*
New York Child Learning Institute (NYCLI) (Queens)
New York Institute for Special Education (Bronx)
New York School for the Deaf (White Plains)
New York State AHRC NYC Chapter Day School
Northside Center (Manhattan)
The Parkside School (Manhattan)
Prime Time for Kids (Manhattan)
Queens Society for Autistic Children (QSAC) (Queens)
The Reece School (Manhattan)
Ryken Program at Xaverian High School (Brooklyn)
School for Language and Communication Development (SLCD) -
    (Queens, Long Island)
Shema Kolainu - Hear Our Voices (Brooklyn)
Shield Institute (Queens)
St. Francis de Sales School for the Deaf (Brooklyn)
St. Joseph's School for the Deaf (Bronx)
The Summit School (Queens, Nyack)
United Cerebral Palsy (UCP) (Brooklyn, Queens, Rye Brook,
    Roosevelt)
Variety Child Learning Center (Syosset)
Westchester Exceptional Children's School (North Salem)
Westchester School for Special Children (Eastchester, Hastings,
    Yonkers)
Woodward Children's Center (Freeport)

Independent schools in and around New York City

Aaron School and Aaron Academy (Manhattan)
Academics at Therapy West (Manhattan)
Alpine Learning Group (New Jersey)
Bay Ridge Prep (Brooklyn)
Beekman (Upper grades) (Manhattan)
Bonim Lamokom - *parochial* (Brooklyn)
Brooklyn Autism Center (BAC) (Brooklyn)
Cahal - *parochial* (Long Island)
Carmel Academy - *parochial* (Connecticut)
Children's Academy (Manhattan)

Columbia Grammar Learning Resource Center (LRC)(Manhattan)
Cooke Center School and Academy (Manhattan)
The Craig School (New Jersey)
David Gregory School (New Jersey)
Deron School (New Jersey)
Dwight Quest Program (Manhattan)
Eagle Hill School - (Connecticut); (*upper grades* - Massachusetts)
ECLC (New Jersey)
The ELIJA School (Long Island)
Forman School - *upper grades* (Connecticut)
The Forum School (New Jersey)
The Foundation School (Connecticut)
Fusion Academy - *upper grades* (Manhattan, Brooklyn, Westchester)
Gan Yisroel - *parochial* (Brooklyn)
Gateway School of New York (Manhattan)
Gersh Academy (Queens and Long Island)
Happy Hour 4 Kids (Manhattan)
The IDEAL of Manhattan (Manhattan)
The International Academy of Hope (iHOPE) (Manhattan)
Imagine Academy (Brooklyn)
IVDU - *parochial* (Brooklyn)
The Kildonan School (Amenia)
Kulanu Academy at HAFTR - *parochial* (Long Island)
The John A. Coleman School (Yonkers)
The Lang School (Manhattan)
The Legacy Program at Xaverian High School (Brooklyn)
Lindamood Bell - *Note: not a school, but a full-time tutorial program*
Manhattan Childrens Center (MCC) (Manhattan)
Manhattan Day - *parochial* (Manhattan)
Manhattan Star Academy (Manhattan)
Maplebrook School (Amenia)
Mary McDowell Friends School (MMFS) (Brooklyn)
McCarton School and Center (Manhattan)
P'TACH - *parochial* (Brooklyn, Manhattan)
The Quad Preparatory School (Manhattan)
Reach for the Stars Learning Center (Brooklyn)
The Rebecca School (Manhattan)
Riverview School - *upper grades* (Massachusetts)
Robert Louis Stevenson School (The Stevenson School) - *upper grades* (Manhattan)
The Shefa School - *parochial* (Manhattan)
SINAI Schools - *parochial* (New Jersey)
The Smith School (Manhattan)

Stephen Gaynor School (Manhattan)
The Sterling School (Brooklyn)
Vincent Smith School (Port Washington)
West End Day School (Manhattan)
The Windward School (White Plains and Manhattan)
Winston Preparatory School - *middle and high school* (Manhattan, Connecticut)
Yeshiva Education for Special Students (YESS) - *parochial* (Queens)
York Prep Jump Start Program - *middle and high school* (Manhattan)

Preschool Pendency

DEFINITION

When a parent disagrees with the recommendation made at their Turning Five CSE Review Meeting, their recourse is to file for an Impartial Hearing. During the course of this hearing and any subsequent appeal the child shall remain in the last-agreed-to placement and the last-agreed-to IEP shall govern. The DOE will pay for their placement during the hearing and/or any appeal.

Stay Put in the child's last agreed to placement during the hearing and/or appeal.

"Order of pendency" issued on first day of hearing.

LIMITATIONS

- The preschool/SEIT agency/related service providers must agree to accept an "order of pendency."
- Expires the following June 30th, even if the child has a 12 month IEP.
- Some limitations on transportation may apply.
- No guarantee that in the school year following the pendency year the child will be permitted to enter a public school kindergarten.

CHAPTER FOUR

Pendency

Remember Jack from Chapter Two? Let's go back and visit with him in order to fully understand the term "pendency" and how it applies to a child who is turning five.

Jack was born at 11:30 pm on December 31, 2011. He was planned as a Valentine's gift, but came prematurely as a New Year's Eve surprise. Immediately following his birth he went into respiratory distress, and had to spend the first four weeks of his life in the NICU. When Jack was released from the hospital, he immediately received Early Intervention (EI) services at home. Although he made noteworthy progress over his first three years, by the time he aged out of EI, his language, motor, and social skills were still behind those of his peers. Everyone believed that Jack was an intelligent little boy, but his issues were persistent, pronounced, and limited his ability to show his true intelligence.

When Jack transitioned from EI into CPSE he was recommended for a 25 hour per week therapeutic preschool. The CPSE referred to the school as a center-based program. While in school, Jack received a total of nine 30-minute sessions per week of related services (OT, PT, ST). The therapists providing the services were school staff and in close contact with his teachers and parents. The DOE funded the entire program, including the round-trip transportation in a mini bus.

After six weeks of attending this preschool, Jack's parents realized that the program was not sufficient. He could not keep up with the increased demands and expectations of the school program. When Jack felt frustrated or overwhelmed, he would have a behavioral regression, which initially occurred at school, but eventually happened at home as well. His parents sought advice from the developmental pediatrician who was following Jack since birth as well as Jack's former EI providers. Everyone encouraged his parents to return to the CPSE coordinator and request a home program in addition to the center-based preschool. The director of the preschool agreed with this recommendation and told the parents that she would strongly support their request for a supplemental home-based program.

Armed with documentation and using all of their advocacy skills, Jack's parents convinced the CPSE coordinator to add an additional 7 hours a week of a home-based program. The program consisted of one hour a day of a SEIT working with him in his home, as well as one hour a week of speech therapy, and one hour a week of occupational therapy at a sensory gym. This was in addition to his continuing attendance at his center-based school. Within a few weeks, Jack was back on track, the behavioral problems diminished, and he was once again making steady progress. When his *parents calculated the cost of this 12-month program, they nearly fainted because it was over $85,000. There is no way they could have afforded to pay this.*

The weeks and months that Jack was receiving this dual program were quickly passing. Jack's progress was notable but his parents were constantly worrying that this program would end in August of 2016 regardless of his young age and developmental delays. Every professional working with Jack said that he was not ready to leave preschool and recommended another year of preschool. Yet his parents knew that this was irrelevant to the DOE who would recommend a kindergarten program based solely on Jack's year of birth. What should his parents do? What are their options?

Here's the good news: If Jack's parents disagree with the turning-five IEP and program recommended by the CSE review team they can challenge the CSE's determination by filing for an Impartial Hearing. Once his parents (generally through an attorney) formally file for an Impartial Hearing, Jack would be able to continue to receive his preschool program, which for him is the dual recommendation of a center-based preschool and 7 hours of after-school services, during the course of the Impartial Hearing and any subsequent appeal. The entire program during this time would be fully paid for by the DOE. This happens as a result of a provision in the IDEA known as "Stay Put." Stay Put was designed as a safeguard serving to protect children whose parents find themselves in dispute with their school district.

RULE

Pendency is not a placement option or a program. It is a legal order directing that a child remain in his or her last-agreed-to placement during the course of an Impartial Hearing and any appeal that might follow that hearing. The pendency or Stay Put provision of the statute mandates that the school district continue to fund this placement during this entire process.

The Legal Background of Pendency or Stay Put

During the 1950s and 1960s, baby boomers were entering school systems in unprecedented numbers. This included mainstream or typically developing children as well as the growing sub-group of children with special needs. These special needs children were not treated fairly or equally to their non-disabled peers. Some school districts were actually telling parents that their special needs child could not come to school for a full day. Even worse, some districts were telling parents to keep their child home from school altogether. In the public elementary school that I attended, there was one multi-grade special education class called CRMD, an acronym for "children with retarded mental development." This class was hidden away in the basement of the school. We hardly ever saw these students, who were not allowed to attend assemblies or special school events. These children were not permitted to eat in the lunchroom or play at recess. Clearly, these were not good times for children with disabilities or for their parents.

As a result of these types of circumstances, parent advocacy groups emerged throughout the country. The parents of children with special needs were becoming a powerful political voice, exerting influence in their home states as well as in Washington, DC. These advocacy groups began suing in federal and state courts arguing that separate is not equal. The principle that "separate is not equal," as it applies to education, was first heralded in the 1954 civil rights desegregation case known as Brown v. Board of Education.

In response to the outcry from parents of special needs children, in 1975 Congress passed the Education Handicapped Act (EHA), which later was renamed the Individuals with Disabilities Education Act (IDEA). While it is now officially called the Individuals with Disabilities Education Improvement Act (IDEIA), it is still referred to as the IDEA. At its core, the IDEA is about equal access to an education for all children, including children with educational disabilities. I will not go into any more detail about the statute other than to tell you that it is the most wonderful piece of affirmative legislation protecting the rights of children.

The EHA/IDEA led to a network of federal, state, and city laws all of which protect the educational rights of special needs children and provide them with programs and opportunities. It also gives parents the right to meaningfully participate in the development of their child's IEP. Because this is a federal law granting an entitlement (the entitlement being a free, appropriate public education or "FAPE"), due process rights automatically attach to the statute.

Congress anticipated occasions when a school district and a parent would disagree with the determination made by the CSE as to what constitutes an appropriate IEP and program. In IDEA cases, when a parent disagrees with a determination made by their school district concerning the needs of their child, the following due process rights are available to them: (1) **written notice** of a parent's rights and what is being recommended for their child; (2) an **opportunity to be heard**; (3) an **opportunity for a due process review of any decision by a neutral third party**, such as a mediator or an impartial hearing officer; and (4) the right to **appeal**.

Nothing in law is simple or easy, including Impartial Hearings. Although Impartial Hearings were meant to be a process for a speedy resolution of a dispute, in actuality they can be lengthy and complex legal and technical proceedings. There is documentary evidence, testimony, briefs, oral, and written arguments. A hearing can also lead to one, two, or even three appeals, and the appeal process can drag on for months and sometimes years.

In contemplating the complexity and length of time that could be involved in a due process Impartial Hearing, Congress was faced with the critical question of what happens to the child during the course of the Impartial Hearing and any possible appeal. Displaying great wisdom, and in a noble attempt to protect the child, Congress answered this question by including the following pendency or "Stay Put" provision within the IDEA:

...during the pendency of any proceedings conducted pursuant to the Act, unless the state or local educational agency and the parents otherwise agree a student with a disability shall remain in his or her then current educational placement.

TIP
The term "proceeding" as used in the IDEA means the hearing or appeal.

TIP
What is not specifically stated in this quote, but is implied, is that the last-agreed-to placement, also referred to as the "pendency placement" is funded by the DOE during the Impartial Hearing and any appeal, with no right of recoupment by the DOE if the parents ultimately lose the case.

A due process Impartial Hearing is only available under the IDEA as it pertains to special education law and children who are classified or if a parent has requested classification. It is not available to a parent whose child does not have an IEP or who is not being considered for special education. If the parent of a general education student disagrees with a determination made by their school district, the appropriate course of action would be an appeal to the Commissioner of Education. This type of appeal is beyond the scope of what is discussed in this book.

In cases invoking pendency, it is customary that the hearing request include several paragraphs that specifically request that on the first day of hearing, the IHO issue an order directing the DOE to continue funding the child's last-agreed-to placement during the course of the Impartial Hearing and any subsequent appeal to that hearing. This is not required, but it certainly makes the hearing officer's job a bit easier.

(Chapter Five is devoted to helping you understand what an Impartial Hearing is. It deals with tuition reimbursement, but the venue and process is the same even though the remedy being sought is different.)

There is a required format and specific content that must be part of any Impartial Hearing request. If critical facts are left out of the hearing request these may not be allowed to be raised during the hearing. During the course of the hearing, documentary evidence is submitted and oral testimony is heard. There is both direct and cross-examination of witnesses. A hearing can last one day or many days; there is no set limit to how long it can last. In New York City, hearings generally do not run consecutive days and given the difficulty in coordinating the schedules of the hearing officer, the attorneys and the witnesses, a hearing can often span several months. Often briefs and memorandums of law are written and submitted in support of each party's position. The application of law in these hearings becomes highly fact specific. The role of the expert witness at a hearing is extremely important. Although Impartial Hearings were meant to be less formal procedures than a traditional court trial, over the last decade they have become longer, more complicated, and quite formalized.

Knowing that a parent has a right to an Impartial Hearing is both comforting and frightening. The comfort is knowing that once pendency is invoked, whether a parent ultimately wins or loses, the school district must continue to fund the last-agreed-to program recommendation that appears on the agreed-to IEP during the course of the hearing and possible appeal. Although I already mentioned this, it is worth repeating: *As the law exists today, the school district is not permitted to seek recoupment of the costs they paid for the child's education under an order of pendency even if ultimately the parent loses their case.*

Take a look at the chart on page 61, "NYC Continuum of Special Education Programs," commonly referred to as the "continuum." You will note that there is no option on this continuum called "pendency." This is because *pendency is not a placement.* By now, I hope you all understand that pendency is, in legal terms, an injunction or an order. It is built into the IDEA and it springs into life once an Impartial Hearing request is filed.

> TIP
> _____
> *Never go into any meeting or appointment at the DOE and ask for pendency. Your attorney may instruct you to ask whether your child can receive another year of preschool, but asking a question for the purpose of clarification is very different from making a premature legal demand.*

Let's go back to Jack to learn a little more about the option of "Stay Put" or "pendency."

After learning from other parents of the possibility that Jack could receive another year of his preschool program, his parents consulted with a special education attorney. They then spoke with the director of his preschool who agreed that Jack should and could remain in the preschool for another year. His parents also spoke with his SEIT and the home-based related service providers, all of whom supported this option and were willing to stay on.

Jack's parents visited their home-zoned public school several times, once accompanied by his SEIT, and another time with his speech therapist. They specifically looked at the ICT class and the 12:1:1 class at this school, seriously considering the appropriateness of these programs. Jack's parents were always fully cooperative with any request made by their CSE. They attended all appointments, provided the district with their private evaluations, promptly submitted the requested medical form, and demonstrated their willingness to consider all public school programs.

Jack's parents were well prepared when they attended their Turning Five Review Meeting. Never once did they mention the words "pendency," "Stay Put," or "injunction." At the point in the meeting where a program recommendation was discussed, his mother genuinely asked if there was any way that Jack could remain in his preschool program for another year, particularly in light of his late birth date, his premature birth, his developmental delays, and his overall immaturity.

As expected, the CSE team classified Jack as having a Speech and Language Impairment and, for September, recommended placement at his local public school in the ICT class with related services. His parents noted their disagreement with this recommendation but told the team they would fully cooperate and consider it. The parents specifically said that although they saw the ICT program a few months earlier, and that at that time it was not appropriate for Jack, in light of the team's official recommendation, they would return and revisit the program with Jack's SEIT. (Again note the subtle but very important distinction—Jack's parents are not agreeing to an ICT, they are merely willing to consider it.) The kindly social worker on the review team responded with, "Off the record, we all agree with you, but there is no way we can recommend this…"

A few days after receiving their final notice of recommendation, Jack's parents visited the proposed ICT program, taking copious notes on what they saw, who they spoke with, and why the program was not "reasonably calculated to confer an educational benefit" to Jack. They responded to the official final notice of recommendation reiterating their disagreement and asking once again for another year of a preschool program.

The summer before the start of the school year, the attorney hired by Jack's parents filed a Request for an Impartial Hearing. The first day of the hearing was in late August. At that initial hearing the attorney requested an order directing the DOE to continue the funding of Jack's preschool program as it appeared on the last-agreed-to IEP during *the course of the Impartial Hearing and any possible appeal. The hearing officer did this without question. This order resulted in the preschool, SEIT, and related service providers receiving their payment as soon as the school year began in September. They were not paid for the entire year, but rather on a monthly basis depending on Jack's attendance and the status of the hearing. The second day of the hearing was scheduled for October. There was no way of knowing how long the hearing would last; however, five days of hearing were scheduled from October through January. The DOE put up two witnesses, the psychologist from the CSE review and the assistant principal at the proposed school. The parents put up six witnesses. Although the last day of the actual hearing was in January, because the impartial hearing officer wanted written briefs in lieu of closing statements, she gave the attorneys another month to submit their legal papers. The case officially closed in late February with a written decision from the impartial hearing officer rendered in April. The parents won. The hearing officer agreed that Jack needed another year of preschool.*

All of this time, Jack's preschool placement was completely funded by the DOE regardless of the outcome. It's as simple as that: While the Impartial Hearing was going on and until a final decision was rendered, Jack's preschool placement was considered to be the last-agreed-to placement and the Stay Put order issued in August directed the DOE to continue funding it. Since the parents won, the DOE was required to continue to pay for the placement, SEIT, and home-based related services.

Now imagine for a moment that Jack's parents had lost the Impartial Hearing, and the judge had made a determination that the DOE was right and Jack was ready for kindergarten. There is still plenty of good news for his parents. Within 25 days of receipt of the losing hearing decision, the parents, through their attorney, would start their appeal. The attorney would notify the DOE of their intent to file an appeal the day she received the losing decision. This means that the preschool program would continue to be completely funded by the DOE until the final appeal decision was rendered.

Appeals take a great deal of time. The first appeal of a decision of an impartial hearing officer is an administrative appeal that is filed in Albany with the New York State Department of Education Office of State Review. This generally takes anywhere from two to four months. A second appeal can be taken from the administrative decision by filing a petition in federal district court and this appeal can take two to three years. All this while, the preschool program would still be paid for by the DOE, and the child would continue to receive the last-agreed-to preschool program.

If Jack's parents win the Impartial Hearing, the DOE has the right to file an appeal. However, while the DOE appeals the case, they still have to continue to pay for Jack's preschool program. In my experience, the DOE has never filed an appeal on a winning preschool pendency proceeding. If the parent wins, and the DOE does not appeal the decision, the parent is also entitled to recoup some or all of the legal fees they paid. (See Chapter Five)

In summary, the opportunity for a turning-five child to remain in his or her current preschool program and not start kindergarten in September of the calendar year in which he or she turns five can happen only when an Impartial Hearing request is filed. It is the filing of the hearing request that invokes or triggers pendency, which is a Stay Put order directing the DOE to continue to fund the preschool placement during the course of the Impartial Hearing and any subsequent appeal.

It is possible for a pendency case to settle before the completion of a full Impartial Hearing. However, settlement on pendency cases requires a highly specific and detailed written stipulation of settlement between the parent and school district, which would include allowing the child to remain in his or her preschool placement and assuring that everyone gets paid. These settlements are complicated and payment through them is handled by a different department at the DOE than the one that handles the pendency payments.

There is another, not-as-widely-used way that a parent can obtain another year of preschool without going to a hearing. This only applies to situations where the child is attending a mainstream (non-special education preschool) and the parent only wants services. This requires that a parent states to the DOE that they do not want a FAPE (free appropriate public education) and that they are parentally placing their child at XYZ preschool and will not sue for reimbursement of the tuition. In this instance, the CSE will create what is known as an IESP (Individual Education Service Program) and not an IEP. The CSE will then either find an agency to fill the mandate or issue a voucher known as an RSA (Related Service Authorization). There are serious limitations to going the route of an IESP. The rate paid can be much lower than the preschool SEIT rate. Getting related service providers can also be a challenge.

TIP

Since an IESP does not carry the same rights as an IEP and has serious limitations, it can be a dangerous option for a parent to pursue.

Limitations on Preschool Pendency

Certain limitations may apply when a parent seeks another year of preschool while their case is being litigated under a pendency (Stay Put) order. The first limitation is that not every preschool, SEIT agency, or provider will accept a child under a pendency order. The determination of whether a school, agency, or provider agrees to accept an order of pendency is made solely by the school, agency, or provider themselves. There is no legal way to force anyone to provide services to a child in this situation. Therefore, it is critical that a parent be absolutely certain that the preschool, SEIT agency, and the therapists that constitute the child's preschool program are all willing to accept the order of pendency.

> **TIP**
>
> *If you discover that your existing SEIT agency is unwilling to accept a pendency order, you still have options. The first and easiest option is to change your SEIT to one who works for an agency that is familiar with and willing to accept a pendency order. If you don't want to lose your existing SEIT or provider, discuss your plans with this person and see if he or she is willing to switch to another agency. Lawyers that practice in this area of law know the agencies that are "pendency friendly." The second option is to have your SEIT get paid directly by the DOE, cutting out the need for an agency. Many SEITs are reluctant to do this, fearful of financial risk. The final way is for the parent to pay the SEIT privately and seek reimbursement. This is very expensive.*

> **TIP**
>
> *If your preschool is funded by the DOE and it is unwilling to accept an order of pendency then there is no way to force them to do so. However, you can change preschools if times permits and there is an opening. As long as the new preschool is a special education school and the class your child is in has the same student-to-teacher ratio as the one that appears on your child's preschool IEP, a pendency order should cover the tuition. This area of law is tricky; consult an attorney before signing a contract with a new school.*

Related service providers present other issues. Basically, a parent must ask these therapists if they are willing to accept an RSA for another year of services.

Another important limitation of pendency involves the time period covered by the pendency order, stipulation, or decision. A pendency order, stipulation of settlement, or a winning hearing decision covers one school year. For a turning-five student this means that pendency ends on June 30th. *A pendency order does not extend through the following summer, even if a child has a 12-month CPSE IEP.*

RULE

A child is considered a "school-age student" based solely on the calendar year in which he or she was born. For all school-age students, whether they have a ten or twelve-month IEP, the school year ends June 30th.

For a school-age child who is recommended for a 12-month program, the school year runs from July 1st through the following June 30th. For a student who attends a 10-month program, the school year runs from September through June 30th. The elementary school-age calendar is different from the calendar for a preschool student. This is all very complicated but all that you have to remember is that a pendency order and its funded services terminate on June 30th of the school year for which it was filed.

TIP

Extending your child's preschool program through the following summer involves another pendency hearing.

In all cases where pendency is invoked, it is important for a parent to have a strong underlying case. The underlying case consists of the reasons that the parent disagrees with the decisions being made by the CSE. Those reasons must be supported by experts and the reports that were submitted to the CSE at the time the determination was made, which means at the Turning Five Review Meeting.

TIP

You must always be fully cooperative with the CSE process. This means attending all meetings, making your child available for evaluations if requested, submitting private evaluations, and doing your due diligence by visiting any proposed placement and fully exploring all of the public school options.

TIP

Expert witnesses win hearings and are critical in any case against a school district. Make sure all of your experts are willing to testify under oath at an Impartial Hearing and are willing to speak to your attorney prior to the hearing in order to prepare. If for some reason a private evaluator tells you that they will not testify at a hearing, this is serious and generally means that it is time to find another evaluator or expert.

Below is an example of what I mean by a strong underlying case. In a hearing request, this summary would be supported by more details, including references to the reports prepared by the evaluator and related service providers, which were given to the CSE in advance of the Turning Five Review Meeting.

Jack's parent claimed that the CSE was wrong in making a determination for him based solely on the fact that he was born in 2011. The parent maintained that this rule was arbitrary and capricious and that given Jack's late birth date, prematurity, and his serious developmental delays, it should not apply to him. All the evaluations and reports before the CSE supported this position. The parent maintained that Jack needed another year of preschool before he would be able to enter a kindergarten class such as the one being proposed for him. Furthermore, after visiting the proposed program, the parent maintained that the class was not reasonably calculated to confer a benefit upon him. The school environment was wrong for Jack and would put him at a serious risk of regression, not progression. The actual school building was too large and over-stimulating. The proposed class was also too large and did not provide Jack with enough individualized attention. The determination to reduce the frequency and length of time of the related services was equally wrong and not supported by any of the evaluations that the review team relied upon at the Turning Five Review Meeting that were prepared by his then-current providers. The complete obliteration of his home-program was not supported by clinical determinations and, again, was contrary to the opinions of all of the professionals who had familiarity with Jack.

This is an outline of the reasons why the hearing was being requested, resulting in the DOE denying Jack a FAPE. The parent is asking the hearing officer to hear the facts, understand the law, and then make the determination by applying the facts to the law. The parent is asking the hearing officer to make a determination of who is right and who is wrong. If the impartial hearing officer finds that Jack's parent is right, then the hearing officer should order the DOE to fund another year of the program which appears on the preschool IEP, and which is reasonably calculated to confer a benefit to him. While this hearing is going on, since the preschool IEP and home program were the last-agreed-to IEP and placement, it must be funded under the Stay Put provision of the IDEA.

Understand, there is a subtle but important distinction in this example. The parents are not seeking pendency as their relief, they are seeking a determination that the program recommended by the CSE review team was inappropriate and wrong for Jack; and they are also seeking determination that he needs another year of his preschool program funded by the DOE. The fact that the funding of the preschool program is happening while there is an ongoing hearing or appeal is just an excellent by-product for the parents. The pendency order is not a determination of the merits of the case. The determination of the merits is made in the hearing officer's final decision.

TIP
_____

The example given above is just a summary of what would be in a pendency hearing request. The actual request would specifically cite statements made in the evaluations and the reports. This is precisely why these reports are so important.

TIP
_____

The timing of when to actually file for any Impartial Hearing is critical and strategic. A parent is eager to have this resolved sooner than later, but most preschool pendency hearings are not filed until July or August. Waiting is always hard, but patience pays off.

Settlement of Preschool Pendency Cases

You might be wondering why a school district would even bother proceeding to hearing in these types of circumstances since it appears to be a win-win situation for parents. The DOE fully understands this. In some cases, particularly one like Jack's, after the first day of a hearing when the order is issued, they would agree to settle the case without further litigation. There are other cases where the school district believes that the child was ready to enter kindergarten and, as such, chooses to defend their recommendation.

When a school district wants to avoid months of litigation, they will reach out to the parents' attorney and offer to settle the case. Usually in pendency matters it is for full or close to the full cost of the entire program, paid prospectively to the agency and providers. A settlement offer cannot be accepted without the consent of the client. If parents agree to the terms of settlement, a document called a stipulation of settlement is drafted and signed by all the parties.

TIP
_____

In recent years, we have seen an increase in cases involving preschool pendency orders where the DOE insists on going forward, knowing they have a weak case. My opinion is that they are doing this to discourage parents from pursuing what is an expensive option for any school district. I call this the newsroom factor – meaning that the DOE wants the news to hit the streets that it is not easy for a parent to get an extra year of preschool!

Pendency for Older Students

The Stay Put or pendency provision in the IDEA is not limited to a turning-five or a preschool child. It is often used for a school-aged child as well. Let me give you a quick example of how it could be used for an older student:

Jack's 10-year-old sister Molly, after failing in an ICT program, was recommended for a deferral to CBST for a New York State Approved Non-Public School. She was placed at the Summit School, which is an approved school. After two years at this school, Molly was doing very well. As a result of her progress, the CSE wanted to change her program recommendation back to an ICT class. Her parents, teachers, therapists, and the private evaluator, who all followed Molly's progress, disagreed with the CSE's recommendation. But, there was no convincing the CSE that an ICT class was inappropriate. Molly's parents found themselves at an Impartial Hearing. The first thing that the lawyer did on day one of the hearing was to invoke pendency or Stay Put so that while the hearing was going on, Summit was being fully paid for by the DOE. This was reflected in the hearing request that the attorney filed.

When pendency or Stay Put is invoked it is a safety net to avoid any potential harm to a child; it is just as invaluable for school-aged children as it is for those turning five.

CHAPTER FIVE

Due Process Impartial Hearing

In this chapter, I will use the example of Sophie to understand what a due process Impartial Hearing is and how to best prepare for one.

Unlike Jack, our little boy whose parent wanted him to have another year of preschool, Sophie was born one week after her due date on 1/1/11. By the age of two, Sophie's language skills were delayed and her pediatrician recommended an evaluation through Early Intervention (EI). Based on this evaluation, Sophie was diagnosed with an expressive and receptive language delay. She met eligibility criteria and received speech, occupational, and physical therapies, all of which were provided and fully paid for by EI.

When Sophie turned three she transitioned from EI into the Department of Education (DOE) Committee on Preschool Special Education (CPSE). An Individual Education Program (IEP) was developed and she was recommended for, and placed in, an integrated class within a center-based therapeutic preschool. There were a total of fifteen children in Sophie's class, some identified as having special needs and others who were typically developing. The special needs children had IEPs, and their programs, which included their related services, were fully funded by the DOE.

In the summer of 2015, before entering her final year of preschool, Sophie's parents had her evaluated by Dr. S., the same neuropsychologist who evaluated her friend Jack. At the time of the evaluation, Sophie was too young for extensive academic testing, but nonetheless the results of the preliminary evaluation indicated that she had many signs of a learning disability, including limited attention span and language processing delays. Dr. S. believed that at the time of testing each of Sophie's delays on their own were mild. However, in combination they would significantly impact her school functioning. Dr. S. recommended a highly specialized school for children with average to above-average intelligence who also have language-based learning disabilities.

In the fall of 2015, Sophie's parents toured and applied to the following schools: Churchill, Gateway, Mary McDowell, Stephen Gaynor, and Windward. The applications were accompanied by the private evaluation as well as progress reports from Sophie's related service providers and her preschool.

Luckily, Sophie was accepted at all five schools. After great deliberation, her parents chose Churchill. What influenced their decision was the fact that Churchill is a NY State Approved Non-Public School (NPS) meaning that for some students, the tuition is directly paid by the DOE. Another consideration was that Churchill starts in kindergarten and goes through twelfth grade. The most important factor in making

Impartial Hearing for Tuition Reimbursement

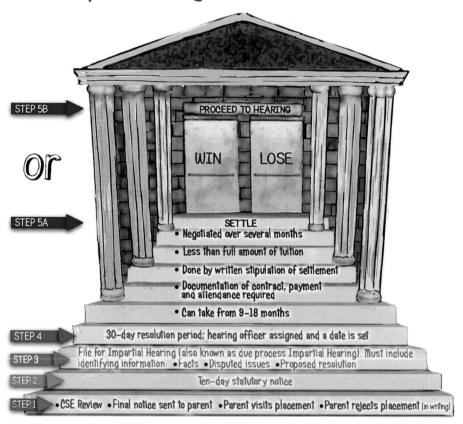

STEP 5B → PROCEED TO HEARING

WIN   LOSE

or

STEP 5A →

SETTLE
- Negotiated over several months
- Less than full amount of tuition
- Done by written stipulation of settlement
- Documentation of contract, payment and attendance required
- Can take from 9–18 months

STEP 4 → 30–day resolution period; hearing officer assigned and a date is set

STEP 3 → File for Impartial Hearing (also known as due process Impartial Hearing). Must include identifying information: • Facts • Disputed issues • Proposed resolution

STEP 2 → Ten-day statutory notice

STEP 1 → • CSE Review • Final notice sent to parent • Parent visits placement • Parent rejects placement (in writing)

their choice was that the overwhelming majority of Churchill graduates attend four year colleges. Sophie's family lived in Brooklyn and were aware that there was a chance she would not be eligible for busing. They decided that Sophie's attending Churchill was worth adjusting their schedules to transport her to and from school.

In February of Sophie's last year of preschool, Churchill sent her parents an enrollment contract for September 2016 admission. The contract required a non-refundable deposit within two weeks of receipt. Although Sophie was known to the CPSE, by February the only contact her parents had from the CSE was a form letter asking for consent to evaluate, a questionnaire, and a request for reports or updates. There was no indication of when the Turning Five Review Meeting would actually occur. Her mother heard from other parents that the review meetings generally took place between March and June.

The attorney that the parents consulted informed them that there was no guarantee that the CSE would defer Sophie's case to the Central Based Support Team

(CBST) for placement and funding at a NY State Approved Non-Public School (NPS). They were warned that they should be prepared to pay the full Churchill tuition and then sue for tuition reimbursement. This would be the same process had Sophie enrolled at Gateway, Gaynor, McDowell, or Windward. The parents understood the risks involved and were willing to proceed.

The parents also knew that if the CSE failed to make a written placement offer by June 15, Sophie might be eligible for a "Nickerson Letter," which could provide funding for one school year. Because of this possibility, the parents saved not only all correspondences from the DOE, but also the envelopes in which they arrived. They also learned that as of the fall of 2013, the DOE stopped automatically issuing Nickerson Letters.

Sophie's Turning Five Review Meeting occurred in April at their local home-zoned public school. The team classified Sophie as having a Speech or Language Impairment and recommended an Integrated Co-Teaching (ICT) kindergarten class with the related services of speech and occupational therapies. Everyone agreed that Sophie no longer needed physical therapy and this was removed from her IEP. As hard as the parents and their attorney tried, there was no way they could convince the review team that Sophie needed a private special education school. It felt like the members of the team had made up their minds even before the meeting began.

Sophie's parents visited the specific placement that the district recommended, which was an ICT class in their local public school. They brought Sophie's current speech therapist with them. The parents had a good relationship with the principal and staff at the school as this was the school that their older son attended. After visiting an ICT class, it was painfully obvious that this type of class would not be appropriate for Sophie. The class was too large and Sophie would never be able to follow directions or keep up with the work. Furthermore, they were told by the teacher that there was no individualized instruction and that all academic work was done in groups.

During this visit, the parents and speech therapist met with the school social worker and the parent coordinator. The parents offered copies of Sophie's private evaluation and the IEP but neither person wanted to look at these. When the parents asked how the school and ICT program would meet Sophie's needs, they were given vague, noncommittal answers.

After the visit, the parents responded to the final notice by writing a detailed letter to the placement officer, who was the person listed on the front page of the final notice form. In their letter they explained why the ICT program was not appropriate for Sophie. They requested a small class placement. To their surprise, at the end of June they received a second notice of placement. This second notice recommended a 12:1:1 class at another public school near their home. Prior to receiving this second notice, there was no second review, no conversation between Sophie's parents and the CSE, and no new IEP was created or sent. All that happened was that they received a different placement offer.

Sophie's mother promptly visited this second placement, this time bringing an educational consultant recommended by a friend. At this second school, they met with the Assistant Principal (AP) in charge of special education. This person spent time reviewing the private evaluation and promptly told Sophie's parents that she was surprised the CSE recommended a 12:1:1 class. The AP claimed that 12:1:1 classes were for lower-functioning students. The other students in the 12:1:1 were intellectually disabled and some had no functional language. The AP made it clear that if Sophie were to attend "her" school, she would immediately change the placement to an ICT class with 24 students and two teachers, not unlike the one that was initially recommended at their local home-zoned school. After her visit to this school, Sophie's mother wrote to the placement officer, explaining why they could not accept the 12:1:1 placement. In her letter she specifically referenced what was said to her by the AP. This time there is no response from the DOE.

The Churchill School required payment in full before the start of the school year. The CSE refused to defer Sophie's case to the Central Based Support Team (CBST) for an NPS placement, leaving her parents with no choice but to pay the full tuition at Churchill and proceed to an Impartial Hearing seeking tuition reimbursement.

There was no news from the DOE over the summer. The parents sent the lawyer all their documents and summaries of their visits and conversations. In the third week of August, the parents' attorney filed a Statutory Notice. The DOE responded with a form letter that stated that they were not inclined to settle the case and that if the parents wanted to pursue the matter they could file for an Impartial Hearing. On September 6th, Sophie began at the Churchill School. Her transition was seamless, she was happy at the school and her teachers were happy with her adjustment.

By the middle of September, the parents' attorney filed an Impartial Hearing request. The request was five pages long detailing the facts and why they disagreed with the IEP and programs offered. There was a specific section in the hearing request entitled "Proposed Resolution" in which the lawyer offered three options: (1) issuing a "Nickerson Letter"; (2) reconvening the CSE for the purpose of deferring the case to CBST for Non-Public School placement back-dated to the first day of school; or (3) reimbursing the parents for the tuition paid to Churchill for the entire school year.

The case was assigned to an impartial hearing officer (IHO) and the hearing was scheduled to begin in the middle of October. The parents' attorney tried to settle the case with a deferral to CBST during a resolution session, but the district refused to do this. However, the DOE did agree to provide busing, making life easier for Sophie's parents.

An attorney from the DOE was assigned to represent the CSE at the hearing. The parents' attorney specifically asked the DOE attorney how she could defend the 12:1:1 placement in light of what was told to the parents by the Assistant Principal during their June visit. The DOE attorney informed the parents' attorney that her client (the DOE) was unwilling to settle and that they believed that the parents never had any intention of enrolling Sophie in a public school. The parents' attorney responded that this was untrue and had either program been appropriate they would have happily used it.

As the October hearing date drew near, Sophie's parents had increasing anxieties. They were assured by their attorney that their case was strong, but they also knew that there was no guarantee. They could afford the first year of tuition at Churchill, but this cost depleted their savings. So much was riding on this hearing; it was no wonder they had trouble sleeping.

Historical and Legal Background

Before continuing with Sophie and her parents, I want to provide some historical and legal background in order to understand the Impartial Hearing process.

A body of law is made up of **Statutes** (also referred to as Acts), **Rules and Regulations** (which provide direction as to how to implement the statute), as well as **Case Law** (which determines whether the cases and regulations were properly applied to a specific case and set of facts).

Think of a statute and regulations as the skeleton of the body. The case law is the muscles, organs, and soul of that body. Case law is law established in the written decisions issued by a court regarding a specific trial, hearing, or review. In reaching and writing a decision, a judge applies the statute, regulations, and prior case law to the specific facts of the immediate case before the court. The concept of applying case law from a prior case to a current case is called "stare decisis," also referred to as "legal precedent." The beauty of having a legal system like ours, which relies so heavily on case law, is that it is dynamic and evolving, reflecting the changing needs of our society. New case law is created throughout our country every day.

The specific federal statutes that govern special education law are the *Individuals with Disabilities Education Improvement Act* (*IDEIA but referred to as the IDEA*), *Section 504 of the Rehabilitation Act of 1973* (*Section 504*), *No Child Left Behind* (*NCLB*), *Family Education Rights to Privacy Act* (*FERPA*), *and the Americans with Disabilities Act* (*ADA*). For the purposes of this book I will focus only on the IDEA and some of the case law generated from this statute.

Now for some history to help in understanding how the IDEA evolved. In 1954, the United States Supreme Court decided the landmark case of <u>Brown v. Board of Education</u> (*347 U.S. 483 [1954]*). This civil rights case paved the way for school desegregation, creating the principle that in education *separate is not equal*. Quoting from this case: "*...in these days it is*

Tuition Reimbursement:
How to Win at an Impartial Hearing

PARENT (We have to meet all three)

Must satisfy and meet all 3 prongs of the test 1 + 2 + 3

1. No offer of FAPE.

and

2. Private placement is calculated to confer a benefit.

and

3. Equities weigh in favor of the parent.

Only when all three prongs are satisfied does a parent **WIN!**

SCHOOL (They have the "ors")

1. If the School District can establish Prong One – They offered FAPE.
   THEY WIN!

or

2. If School District did not provide FAPE, but the school district through cross-examination of the parent's witnesses can establish the private school is not appropriate.
   THEY WIN!

or

3. If the School District did not provide FAPE, the private school was appropriate for the child BUT the equitable considerations did not weigh in favor of the parents.
   THEY WIN!

doubtful that any child may reasonably be expected to succeed in life if he is denied the opportunity of an education. Such an opportunity, where the State has undertaken to provide it, is a right which must be made available to all on equal terms..." It is easy to see the path being laid for our special education students.

Nine years later, in 1965, Congress passed the *Elementary and Secondary Education Act*, which provided states with resources so that disadvantaged students would have access to quality education. In 1966, this law was amended to provide a grant program to help improve programs for the education of handicapped children.

The early 1970s saw lawsuits filed in federal courts throughout the country. These suits were brought by parents of special needs children, alleging that disabled students were not being provided with an education equal to their non-disabled peers, and were thus being denied equal protection and due process under the law. The two leading cases that argued this point were <u>Pennsylvania Association for Retarded Children v. Commonwealth of Pennsylvania</u> ("PARC") and <u>Mills v. Board of Education of District of Columbia</u> ("Mills"). PARC concerned children with intellectual disabilities who were being excluded from public schools and Mills dealt with children with disabilities who were suspended, expelled, or excluded from public schools in the District of Columbia.

As a result of these cases, in 1972 Congress launched a full investigation into the status of the education that was being provided to children with disabilities. This investigation revealed horrible statistics: In 1972, there were over 8 million children in the United States with handicapping conditions who required special education. However, only 3.9 million children were receiving an appropriate education, while 2.5 million children were receiving an inappropriate education, and 1.75 million children were receiving no educational services at all.

In 1973, which was around the same time that this congressional investigation was occurring, Congress passed *Section 504 of the Rehabilitation Act of 1973.* We refer to this as "Section 504." This is the first civil rights statute in the United States for people with disabilities. As it pertains to education, this statute broadly prohibits students from being denied participation in or enjoyment of the benefits offered by public school programs because of a student's disability.

As a direct result of the congressional investigation of 1972, and on the shoulders of Section 504, in 1975 Congress enacted *The Education for All Handicapped Children Act*, also known as Public Law 94-142, which was reauthorized and renamed in 1990 as the *Individuals with Disabilities Education Act (IDEA)*, and in 2004 revised and renamed as the *Individuals with Disabilities Education Improvement Act (IDEIA)*. We still refer to this statute as the IDEA.

The IDEA is known as "spending clause" legislation. Simply put, if a state agrees to accept federal funding for special education programs then the state's education agency must adhere to the provisions of the IDEA and its implementing regulations. The IDEA requires that school districts evaluate children who are suspected of having educational handicapping conditions. If the child is found eligible, the school district is responsible for creating an individualized educational program (IEP) with parental input. This program is to provide an educational experience for the child that is as close as possible to the educational experience of their non-disabled peers. The IDEA places a significant emphasis on the meaningful participation of parents in the development of their child's educational program.

The four major goals of the IDEA are: (1) to ensure that special education services are available to children who need them; (2) to guarantee that decisions about services to disabled students are fair and appropriate; (3) to establish specific management and auditing requirements for special education; and (4) to provide federal funds to help the states educate students with disabilities.

The concept that a school district must offer a student who is identified as having an educational handicap a Free Appropriate Public Education, (FAPE), is the cornerstone of the IDEA. When a parent believes that the decisions and actions of their school district have denied their child a FAPE, their recourse is to file a request for mediation or an Impartial Hearing.

Prior to 1975 and the passing of the EHA, if a parent disputed a decision made by their school district pertaining to the education of their "educationally handicapped" child, their only recourse was to proceed directly into court under the Rehabilitation Act of 1973. This type of legal proceeding was cumbersome and expensive. With the passing of the EHA/IDEA there is a requirement in the statute requiring school districts to have administrative procedures that a parent can use, free of charge, if they dispute any decision made about their child's education. These procedures are either Mediation or an Impartial Hearing.

TIP

In NYC tuition reimbursement cases can never be resolved at mediation, therefore for purposes of this chapter I will focus only on an Impartial Hearing.

The pivotal question at every Impartial Hearing seeking tuition reimbursement or direct funding for an approved private school is whether or not the DOE/CSE offered a child a FAPE.

TIP
_____

*Whether you do your own hearing or use an attorney, make sure
that in your hearing request there is an explicit statement that the
DOE denied your child a FAPE.*

In trying to answer the threshold question of whether a child is offered a FAPE, an impartial hearing officer and any subsequent appeal court will first turn to the official definition of FAPE found in the statute. The IDEA defines FAPE as: *"Special Education and Related Services that: (A) have been provided at public expense...without charge [to the parents]; (B) meet the standards of the State Educational Agency; (C) include an appropriate preschool, elementary, or secondary school education in the State involved; and (D) are provided in conformity with the student's Individualized Education Program."*

This is a vague definition that offers no guidance as to what specific standard or level of learning and achievement must be met in order to determine if FAPE was offered. The important question of what is appropriate for a specific child is what I refer to as the "litigated itch." Because of the lack of clarity in the statute, impartial hearing officers and appeal courts turn to the case law for guidance in defining FAPE.

Leading Special Education Cases

Board of Ed. of Hendrick Hudson Central School District v. Rowley, 458 U.S. 176 (1982)("Rowley")

This is the first IDEA case heard by the U.S. Supreme Court after the passing of the EHA. In this early decision, the court attempted to define and set standards for what is a FAPE. As with all special education cases, Rowley began at an Impartial Hearing and worked its way up through the federal courts.

The parents of student Amy Rowley argued that FAPE required their school district to maximize the potential of handicapped children commensurate with the opportunities offered to all other children. Unfortunately, the court did not agree with the parents and instead held that the EHA (now the IDEA) did not require schools to proportionally maximize the potential of handicapped students. The Supreme Court interpreted that the intent of the EHA was to open the doors of public education to handicapped children by means of specialized educational services; it did not guarantee any particular substantive level of education once inside. FAPE is satisfied when the IEP is reasonably calculated to enable a child to receive an educational benefit, which only means "some educational progress." The Rowley standard or definition of FAPE is a low standard and is still the law of the land and cited in every special education case.

TIP
One thing we have all learned from Rowley is that a CSE does not have to offer the best program or a program that would maximize your child's potential. Therefore you should never ask for the "best" program. Instead, ask for an "appropriate" program when referring to what you want from your school district for your child.

TIP
Since the school district's burden is low, it is essential that if you find yourself at an Impartial Hearing that you have an expert witness to poke holes in the DOE's case. Expert witnesses are essential in proving that a proposed program is not appropriate for a specific child. Hearings are won by experts!

Irving Independent School District v. Tatro, 468 U.S. 883 (1984)

This is the next major decision issued by the U.S. Supreme Court, dealing with the EHA (IDEA). This decision addressed the definition of related services.

In this case, the student, Amber Tatro, is diagnosed with cerebral palsy. In order for her to attend school she needs to be catheterized every few hours. Her school district agreed to provide special education for Amber, however, they refused to do the catheterization, claiming this was a medical need and not educational. This landmark case addressed the scope of related services and created what is referred to as the medical exception rule. *A school district must provide all supportive services necessary for a student to attend school and receive an education, unless a physician is needed to provide the service.* Since a nurse could change a catheter, the district was ordered to do this for Amber as an educationally related service.

Burlington School Committee v. Massachusetts Department of Education, 471 U.S. 359 (1985) ("Burlington")

This landmark decision is cited in every special education tuition reimbursement case. It establishes a parent's right to sue for tuition reimbursement and sets forth the test that must be used in determining whether or not parents are eligible for tuition reimbursement. It also set the groundwork for the "Carter" decision.

In Burlington, the parent of a third grade special education/IEP student, Michael, believed that his son's learning disabilities were not adequately addressed by the IEP proposed and provided by his school district (Burlington, Massachusetts). The dispute between Michael's parent and the school district continued throughout the school year, and Michael kept struggling under the existing IEP, which was the subject of the parent's challenge. While the debates and arguments between the parent and the school district continued, the parent decided, without the approval or recommendation of the school district, to remove Michael from the public school and place him in a private special education school that he believed would better address Michael's specific needs. After placing Michael in the private school, the parents sued the town of Burlington for the cost of this program, alleging that the school district had failed to provide Michael with a Free and Appropriate Public Education (FAPE).

The town of Burlington refused to reimburse the parent for the tuition paid for the private school. The district argued that the IEP they offered was appropriate for Michael; they further argued that the father relinquished his right to a due process hearing because he removed Michael from the public school. The school district's position was that Michael had to remain in his public school placement through the duration of the due process hearing in order to be eligible for any possible award of tuition.

This case went on for six years, starting at due process impartial hearing, and travelling through the federal courts until it finally reached the United States Supreme Court in 1985. The Supreme Court overwhelmingly and unanimously ruled in favor of the parent, establishing a parent's right to unilaterally place their child and then sue for reimbursement. Here is some specific language from this landmark case, leading to the Court's decision that the school district was wrong:

> "...if the school officials disagree with the need for special education or the adequacy of the public school program to meet the child's needs, it is unlikely they will agree to an interim private school placement while the review process runs its course, thus the parents are forced to leave the child in what may turn out to be an inappropriate educational placement or to obtain the appropriate placement only by sacrificing any claim for reimbursement."

In the Burlington decision, the Supreme Court created what is known as the **Burlington Three-Prong Test for Tuition Reimbursement**, which is: A parent can unilaterally place their child in a private school and obtain tuition reimbursement if: (1) the school district failed to offer the child a FAPE; (2) the parent's private school placement was reasonably calculated to confer a benefit to the child; and (3) equitable considerations do not constitute a bar to an award of tuition.

The limitation of this case is that it dealt with an "approved" school. However, eight years later, in 1993, the Supreme Court issued a decision that is referred to as the "Carter case" in which the Court expanded the right to seek tuition reimbursement when a child is unilaterally placed in an independent (non-approved) school.

Three-Prong Burlington/Carter Test for Tuition Reimbursement

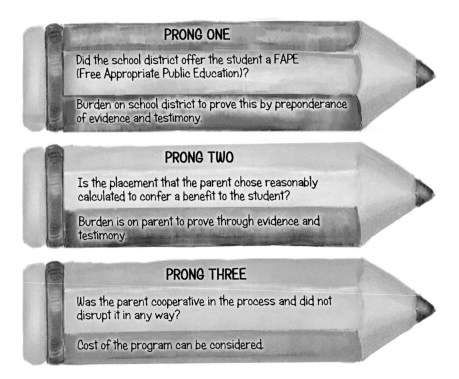

PRONG ONE

Did the school district offer the student a FAPE (Free Appropriate Public Education)?

Burden on school district to prove this by preponderance of evidence and testimony.

PRONG TWO

Is the placement that the parent chose reasonably calculated to confer a benefit to the student?

Burden is on parent to prove through evidence and testimony.

PRONG THREE

Was the parent cooperative in the process and did not disrupt it in any way?

Cost of the program can be considered.

Florence County School District Four v. Shannon Carter, 510 U.S. 7 (1993) ("Carter")

In this case, the parents of Shannon Carter disputed the appropriateness of the proposed placement recommended by their school district. Unlike Burlington, where the school that the parents chose was on a state-approved list, in the Carter case, Shannon attended an independent school. The Supreme Court expanded Burlington to include a placement at an independent school. Simply put, if parents can meet the three-prong test for reimbursement established in Burlington, then they have a right to reimbursement even if the private school they chose is not certified by the State nor complies with all of the IDEA requirements. As a result of this case, the Burlington test for reimbursement is now called the *Three-Prong Burlington/Carter Test for Tuition Reimbursement*.

Honig v. Doe, 484 U.S. 305 (1988)

This is the only case the Supreme Court has ever heard regarding discipline. It removed a school's unilateral authority to suspend or expel a student with an IEP for more than 10 days unless there is evidence of weapons, drugs, or serious bodily injury. The school must get a ruling from a hearing officer or court for suspensions greater than 10 days in any school year.

Cedar Rapids Community School District v. Garret F., 526 U.S. 66 (1999)

Once again, the Supreme Court looked at related services for special needs children and decided that cost is not a factor in determining what is appropriate. If a related service is needed in order for a child to attend a public school and the related service does not meet the "bright line" medical exception test established in Tatro, the school district must provide it.

New York City Board of Education v. Tom F., 552 U.S. 1 (2007)

In this case, the parent (Tom F.) of a child attending the Stephen Gaynor School sued the NYC DOE for tuition reimbursement. The DOE took the position that because the child never attended a public school his parents had no entitlement to seek tuition reimbursement. The basis for the DOE's challenge is a confusing sentence in the IDEA that says the act "...authorizes reimbursement for a child who previously received special education and related services under the authority of a public agency..." This one clause in a sentence was the subject of years of litigation and appeals.

The Supreme Court was tied in its decision because Justice Kennedy recused himself from participating. Because it was a tied decision, it meant that the decision of the lower court, the Second Circuit Court of Appeals, was binding. The Second Circuit ruled in favor of the parents' right to sue for reimbursement even if they had not previously enrolled their child in public school.

These seven cases provide a very brief summary of special education case law. There are hundreds of federal cases that are very important and relevant to attorneys practicing in this field. Parents who are interested in reading these cases and becoming more familiar with the law should join the Council on Parents Attorneys and Advocates (*www.copaa.org*).

What does the term "due process under the law" mean?

This term can be somewhat confusing because "due process" has two meanings. The first meaning refers to a set of rights and protections that a parent has. The second meaning refers to an actual Impartial Hearing.

Let's first talk about the rights and protections that are part of the IDEA. When a statute, such as the IDEA, grants a citizen a "right" or "entitlement" there are inherent protections that automatically attach to the statute. These inherent protections are found in the fifth and fourteenth amendments of the U.S. Constitution and are referred to as "due process under the law."

Due process under the law is a constitutional guarantee that all governmental proceedings, both federal and state, will be fair and not deprive a person of life, liberty, or property. Under the IDEA, due process requires that school districts provide parents with **written notice** as to what their rights are and as to the determinations made by their school district, an **opportunity to be heard**, an **opportunity for review of any decision by a neutral third party,** and an opportunity for **appeal.**

To satisfy the **written notice** requirements, school districts must provide a parent with a publication called "New York State Procedural Safeguards Notice: Rights for Parents of Children with Disabilities, Ages 3-21." This booklet explains what a parents due process rights are. Sometimes it is sent in the mail, and sometimes it is given to parents at the social history meeting prior to the Turning Five Review Meeting. You can read a copy of it online at: *www.p12.nysed.gov/specialed/publications/psgn-cover-jan12.htm.*

In addition, the school district will send parents a document called "Prior Written Notice." This notice comes twice—once after the initial referral and again after the IEP meeting.

Parents have an absolute right to have an **opportunity to be heard,** which entails meaningful participation in the development of their child's IEP and in any other matter that concerns their child's special education.

Parents also have a right to an **opportunity for review of any decision by a neutral third party.** Generally the decisions in question are about a child's eligibility, classification, placement, related services, methodology, or other aspects of the IEP. A parent who wants a decision reviewed may either choose Mediation or an Impartial Hearing.

Mediation

During mediation, the parent and a representative from the school district meet with a neutral third party who tries to help the parties reach an agreement. The mediator is not a judge and has no authority to impose a decision to resolve the disagreement.

TIP

In NYC we do not recommend using mediation for any dispute that has a financial component. Neither the mediators nor the DOE have the authority to order reimbursement under mediation.

Impartial Hearing

There are specific procedures for filing for an Impartial Hearing that must be followed and are provided by the DOE Impartial Hearing Office *(www.p12.nysed.gov/specialed/publications/policy/parentguide.htm)*.

In New York City, an impartial hearing officer must be an attorney, while outside of NYC they can be either an attorney or a former school district official. All hearing officers must take a state-level course, pass an exam, and become certified. They are sometimes referred to as administrative law judges.

Outside of New York, the term "due process" is used to describe what we call an Impartial Hearing. So if someone says they are going to "due process," what they mean is an Impartial Hearing. It is also perfectly correct to refer to an Impartial Hearing as a Due Process Impartial Hearing.

Whoever loses at an Impartial Hearing (either the parent or the school district) has an automatic right to an **appeal** of that decision. The first level of appeal in New York State is the NYS Education Department Office of State Review (SRO). The majority of cases that are lost (by either party) at an Impartial Hearing do not get taken to appeal. In New York State there are approximately 6500 Impartial Hearings filed each year, yet fewer than 250 are taken to appeal at the SRO.

Any party who loses their SRO case has a further right to appeal in state court (NYS Supreme Court) or in the federal court system (Federal District Court). If a party is dissatisfied with the State Supreme Court's decision, an appeal may then be taken to the New York State Appellate Division and then to the New York State Court of Appeals (the New York State Court of Appeals is not obligated to review every appeal).

> **TIP**
> _____
>
> *Seasoned attorneys who practice in the area of special education law rarely, if ever, go into State Court, and instead proceed through the federal court system. The federal courts are more familiar with the IDEA.*

In the federal court system, the first appeal from the SRO is to the Federal District Court, and after that to the Federal Circuit Court of Appeals. If either party is dissatisfied with the result obtained in the Federal Circuit Court of Appeals then there is a right to apply for certiorari to the United States Supreme Court. The U.S. Supreme Court is not obligated to take every case that applies to it and it is relatively difficult to have a case heard by the U.S. Supreme Court.

Now that you have some technical legal background, let's return to Sophie and her nervous parents...

When we left off, Sophie's parents were having sleepless nights awaiting the start of their Impartial Hearing. They understand through their attorney that their case will be heard in front of an impartial hearing officer who will apply the three prongs of the Burlington/Carter Test that were established by the United States Supreme Court.

The Burlington/Carter Test

Prong One: The threshold question asked and analyzed by every impartial hearing officer (IHO) in every tuition reimbursement case is: Did the school district offer this particular student a FAPE? In reaching a determination, the IHO will consider whether the school district complied with the procedural and substantive requirements of the IDEA. This includes whether or not the parent was afforded an opportunity for meaningful participation in the development of

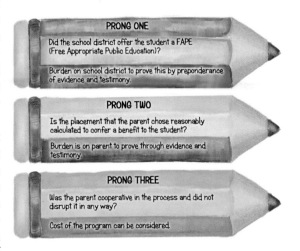

their child's IEP. Did the school district develop an IEP that correctly reflects the abilities and needs of the child? Did the IEP create appropriate goals and ways of measuring the progress of the child in reaching these goals? Are the IEP and program recommended reasonably calculated to confer a benefit to the child?

In New York State, the burden of proof on the first prong of the Burlington/Carter test is with the school district. What this means is that the school district has the responsibility to prove through the evidence and testimony that they offered the child a FAPE.

If the impartial hearing officer is convinced that the IEP is sufficient and the program that the DOE is recommending, although not perfect, is good enough, meaning that it is likely to produce progress and not regression, then there is no need to go further with the three-prong analysis. Technically, the inquiry is over; the school district wins and the parents lose. However, neither the school district nor the parent will know this during the actual hearing. The hearing officer does not make a verbal ruling during a hearing and continues to take evidence and hear testimony concerning the other two prongs of the Burlington/Carter test.

TIP

If you are at a hearing never think that just because a school district failed to defend their IEP placement that you will automatically win. There are two other prongs that are equally important.

Prong Two: The burden of proof now shifts to the parents to prove through evidence and testimony that the private school that they chose for their child was, at the time of enrollment, reasonably calculated to confer a benefit to the child. This prong requires testimony not only from the parent, but also from the private school and the experts involved in the child's life.

Testimony from the private school is generally given by an administrator at the school who presents an overview of the school, talks about the school's educational philosophy and methodology, gives a description of the population served, the credentials of the staff, the curriculum followed, and the techniques used to individualize instruction. There must be someone from the school who can testify with firsthand knowledge about the student, his or her needs, and how the specific program addresses these needs.

TIP

It is critical that the private school is willing to testify at a hearing. If a school is unwilling to testify and the case is at an Impartial Hearing, the parent will have to hire an expert who: (1) is familiar with the school, (2) will visit and observe the child in that school, (3) confer with teachers and administrators, and then (4) testify at the hearing in lieu of the school. Even with this type of expert testimony there are hearing officers that will not find this sufficient, and will rule that because the school did not testify at the hearing the parent has not met their burden under the second prong of Burlington/Carter.

TIP

There are very few schools that refuse to testify; you must know this prior to enrollment at the school and be willing to take the risk.

For a parent to meet their burden under prong two, they must testify about their child's development as well as a detailed chronology of their dealings with the CSE. This testimony will provide fact-specific details about the relevant meetings with the CSE, what materials they provided to the CSE, how they cooperated with the process, what public school programs they considered, and their opinion as to why the CSE's proposed program is not able to meet their child's needs.

TIP
_____
A good lawyer prepares all witnesses including the parent. The preparation, which we refer to as "prep," is to make sure that each witness fully understands the issues and has copies of and is familiar with the reports and documents that will be used and referenced at the hearing. The prep should include a review of the parents direct testimony and what the cross-examination by the DOE attorney will be like.

TIP
_____
Because parents never know at a hearing what the IHO is thinking and what the ruling will be, it is very important that the case is thoroughly prepared on all three prongs. If you are at a hearing and think you have a slam dunk on prong one, do not sit back and relax. Your attorney must still prepare and present testimony and evidence supporting the remaining two prongs. If a parent wins and the DOE takes the case to appeal, the appeals officer can reverse on any prong; so the record must be complete.

There are instances where an impartial hearing officer will find that the DOE failed to meet their prong one burden, but that the school the parents chose is not appropriate, meaning that prong two is not met. This can happen in a number of instances, including when an IEP recommends a related service that the school does not provide, such as speech therapy, occupational therapy, counseling, or physical therapy, and the school does not give sufficient testimony as to how they are meeting the student's needs without this service. Another reason a hearing officer can find a school inappropriate is if it is too restrictive. There must be answers ready if these issues are raised.

Prong Three: This prong is also referred to as **Equitable Considerations.** It is an ambiguous prong, and there is no one variable that has to be met. Attorneys look to the language in the statute and case law for an understanding of equitable considerations. In determining whether this prong has been satisfied in favor of the parent, the IHO will look at the totality of the case. Did the parent do anything to preclude or hamper the CSE process? Did the parent fully cooperate with the CSE? Did the parent make themselves and the child available for all appointments and meetings at the CSE? Did the parent provide the CSE with all evaluations, reports, and assessments? Was the parent truly open to consideration of a public school program? When did the parent sign the contract with the private school, and were they willing to walk away from their deposit? The basic inquiry is whether the parent in any way hindered the CSE's process of developing an IEP and making a program recommendation.

TIP

When trying to understand what an equitable consideration is, think of the word fairness. Ask yourself am I being fair with the DOE? Am I dealing with the CSE with "clean hands"?

The IHO can rule that the DOE did not provide FAPE (prong one) and the school the parent chose for the child was calculated to confer a benefit (prong two), but because of an intentional action or inaction of a parent (like not making a child available for testing, missing appointments, or withholding a second version of a report), will still rule against a parent and deny or limit tuition reimbursement.

Date of the Contract with the Private School

At an Impartial Hearing, the DOE often tries to raise the issue of when the parents signed the contract with the private school. This is done in the hopes of having a hearing officer make a prong three (equitable) determination against the parent. The good news is that case law is on the parents' side. It has been repeatedly held by the courts that the date a parent signs a contract with a private school does not relieve the school district of their responsibility to hold a timely review meeting, create a valid IEP, and make a program recommendation reasonably calculated to confer a benefit.

Even with this case law, the DOE insists on raising this issue at almost every hearing in an effort to establish that the parent had no interest in a public school program. In law we refer to this as "making a negative inference." Lawyers for parents argue strongly against establishing an inference from the date that a contract is signed, claiming that the parent needs a safety net for their child in the event that the DOE does not offer a FAPE. Most private school contracts permit a parent to be released from the contract if they accept a public school placement by a certain date. The schools do hold the parents responsible for a nonrefundable deposit.

TIP

Read the contract from the private school carefully and understand your obligations. If you have questions about the contract, call the school for clarity.

Statutory Notice Requirement

If you remember from our example of Sophie, prior to the attorney filing for an Impartial Hearing in the late summer she filed something referred to as "statutory notice." Filing of this notice is considered a condition precedent to filing for an Impartial Hearing. In all tuition reimbursement cases, there is a requirement that the parents provide the school district with notice: (a) either at the most recent IEP meeting prior to their removal of the child from the public school; or (b) in writing, ten days before removing the child from the public school district.

Notice must include the reasons why they are rejecting the IEP and placement proposed by the school district, and must state their intent to enroll their child in a private school at public expense. The notice must be filed ten business days before placement, which includes any holidays that occur on a business day. Failure to adhere to this notice require-ment can result in reduction in the amount of tuition reimbursement awarded or a complete denial of the tuition reimbursement.

At the end of June 2014, Mayor Bill de Blasio issued an initiative creating a policy where the DOE could settle a tuition reimbursement case on the basis of notice alone. This initiative is not a law and there is uncertainty as to how long it will be in effect.

TIP
Some lawyers will have you write your own notice, while other firms write and file the notice on behalf of their clients. Either way is fine; just make sure the magic words are in the notice!

TIP
The operative word when a notice is not filed or is incomplete is that an IHO "may" reduce or deny tuition. The notice requirement is critically important, but not necessarily a fatal flaw.

TIP
There are situations when notice is not required, but this is very case specific and must be discussed with your attorney.

TIP
The timing of filing the notice is important. Without being specifi-cally directed by your attorney to do otherwise, you should not give notice at your Turning Five Review Meeting if that meeting is held prior to the start of a school year. To do this would give a serious negative inference that the parent has no intention of considering a public school placement.

Impartial Hearing Request
In Sophie's case the DOE did not settle on the basis of notice alone. They responded to the notice by sending a written form letter indicating that they were not

settling and that the parent could proceed by filing for an Impartial Hearing, which is what her lawyer did.

Currently, there is a two-year statute of limitations for filing a hearing request. The statute of limitations runs from the date the parent knew or should have known of the "harm." Most attorneys practicing in this area of law look at this as the date of the CSE review.

The hearing request has specific information that must be included in the caption and in the body of the request. The caption must include the child's name, birth date, home address, telephone number, and the parents' names. If you know the NYC ID number, this should be included too. The body of the hearing request must provide, in detail, the parents' specific disagreements with the IEP and placement. *If an issue or disagreement is not raised in the hearing request, it will not be permitted to be raised at the hearing.* There is a way of amending an insufficient hearing request.

> **TIP**
>
> *Every attorney has their own style of writing. If you are choosing between two or more attorneys, it is appropriate to ask to see a sample of the type of hearing request they write. Some parents request to see a draft of the hearing request prepared by their attorney before it is filed. Again, this is acceptable and often recommended particularly when there are complicated facts.*

In addition to giving the specific nature of the disagreement, or what is known as the disputed issues, the hearing request must also include a section entitled "proposed resolution."

Once the hearing request is filed, it is assigned a case number. The DOE responds with a form entitled "due process response." This is followed by a 30-day resolution period, during which time a resolution meeting between the parents and the school district can occur. Resolution can be waived; it is not mandatory.

> **TIP**
>
> *Resolution is always waived in tuition reimbursement cases, since the DOE has no authority to agree to reimbursement at a resolution meeting. However, in cases seeking other remedies, like a deferral to CBST or a Nickerson Letter, resolution might not be waived unless the parent was specifically told that the district would not offer these remedies.*

A hearing officer is assigned to the case shortly after it is filed. Once the resolution period has expired, a hearing date is set. In some instances the DOE will be represented by an attorney. In other instances it is a lay person from the district who has been designated to represent the district.

In Sophie's case, a lawyer from the DOE was representing the district. Once the parent's attorney learned this, she immediately contacted the DOE attorney in an attempt to settle the case. When the two attorneys finally spoke, the parents' attorney was abruptly told that the DOE would not settle the case and that they wanted to proceed to a hearing.

Settlement

Any way you look at it, and no matter what you choose to call it, an Impartial Hearing is a lawsuit. It is adversarial and unpleasant. Once a hearing request is filed, there are three possible outcomes:

If a parent **wins** it is generally for full tuition for only the school year in question. If a parent wins and the DOE does not appeal, they can recoup some or all of the legal fees paid to their attorney. Additionally, pendency is now established. This is referred to as "pendency on decision." In a situation where the DOE has lost, they have 35 days after the issuance of the written decision to file an appeal with the State Review Officer. This means that for 35 days after winning, a parent is still holding their breath, hoping that there will be no appeal.

If a parent **loses** unfortunately, this means they lose all—there is no reimbursement for the tuition for that year, there is no entitlement to reimbursement of attorney fees, and pendency is not established. If a parent loses at an Impartial Hearing, they have the same right to file for an appeal with the State Review Office. A parent (generally through their attorney) must file "Notice of Intention to Seek Review" within 25 days of the date of the decision. Ten days later they must file the full petition, usually accompanied by a memorandum of law.

The third option after filing for an Impartial Hearing is **settlement**. Settlement of a case means that a parent does not receive all that they have sought, meaning that they do not receive full tuition reimbursement or reimbursement of legal fees, and pendency is not established; however they do not risk everything because they do receive some agreed upon amount. In all areas of law, not only special education, settlement occurs in the vast majority of cases.

Although most parents would readily agree to a settlement, the only party that can recommend a settlement is the party being sued, in Sophie's case that means the school district.

If the school district agrees to settle a case, it is highly unusual that it will be for full tuition reimbursement. I have kept statistics on settlement on my firm's tuition reimbursement cases from 1993 through 2013.

Each year during these twenty years, 88 to 92 percent of all cases settled at a rate between 80 and 90 percent of the actual cost of tuition. Of course, there are exceptions at both ends of this range, specific to the facts of the case. If a parent receives a scholarship, the actual cost of tuition is reduced. The DOE negotiates settlement on what the parent was actually responsible for paying.

There is no formula used by the DOE in determining what the rate of settlement on a specific case will be. There are over a dozen lawyers and paralegals at the DOE whose jobs are to negotiate settlements. The cases are randomly assigned. Each person at the DOE has their own system and approach to settlement. It is not unusual for two different children with similar facts to have two disparate settlement offers. It varies based on who is negotiating for the DOE.

The advantage of a settlement is that a parent receives a substantial portion of the school tuition, with no risk of losing at a hearing—or even worse sitting through days and months of a hearing, winning, and then having the DOE appeal the case, only for the parent to lose on appeal.

TIP

Remember my hero, Winston Churchill, who said, "A bad peace is always better than a good war!"

If the DOE believes that they have developed a good IEP with appropriate goals, and they recommended a program that they believe can meet the needs of the child, then they will proceed to an Impartial Hearing.

As a result of Mayor de Blasio's June 2014 Special Education Initiative, the settlement process radically changed. For the 2014-2015 school year, close to 95% of all cases settled with a higher settlement rate than ever before. Some cases even went as high as 100%.

TIP

The 2014-2015 school year was the first year in which we saw a major increase in both the number of cases being recommended for settlement and the rate at which they settled. This must be viewed with caution.

The Actual Hearing

Let's return to Sophie, whose case was not recommended for settlement. Sophie's Impartial Hearing was scheduled for late October. Her parents met with their lawyer and were thoroughly prepared for the hearing. Sophie's mother would testify as the last witness and would meet with the attorney right before giving her testimony in order to prepare in great detail.

TIP
_____

Having a parent as the last witness at an Impartial Hearing is a common litigation strategy. The parent has heard all the prior testimony, knows the DOE position, and has a sense of what questions their testimony should address.

On the first day of hearing, the parents met with their attorney an hour before the hearing in the waiting room at the Impartial Hearing Office, which is located at 131 Livingston Street in Brooklyn. Due to the high volume of cases, they waited for over an hour just to be assigned to a hearing room and court reporter.

TIP
_____

It is not unusual to wait for a room and reporter. You must be prepared for this.

The hearing room is about the size of a small conference room (or a large walk in closet). Some of the hearing rooms have windows but most do not. There is a conference table in the middle of the room with several microphones. At one end of the table sits the impartial hearing officer (IHO), and at the other end sits the court reporter, wearing headphones and monitoring a recording device which creates an official record and transcript. The parents and their attorney sit on one side of the table and the DOE lawyer and a district representative sit at the other side of the table. The room is crowded and doesn't look anything like the courtrooms the parents have seen on television. There is barely room at the table for everyone's notebook and the stacks of legal papers.

By 11:00 a.m., the hearing finally began. The DOE attorney arrived with a person that the parents vaguely recall meeting at their Turning Five Review Meeting. Before anyone introduced themselves, the hearing officer announced, "Before going on the record [which means before turning the recording device on], I have to stop the hearing no later than 2:00 p.m." The person sitting with the DOE attorney immediately chimed in, "Well I have to leave by 1:00 pm, and furthermore because I have low blood sugar I must eat lunch no later than 12 noon." The parents' lawyer immediately objected to the taking of testimony from this person if she was unable to remain for cross-examination. The judge agreed, and decided that under the circumstances the first day of the hearing would only deal with the submission of evidence, scheduling of subsequent hearing dates, exchanging lists of witnesses and, if time permitted, opening statements made by both attorneys.

When the DOE representative heard this she jumped up, grabbed her folder, and announced, "In that case, I am going back to my school." Out the door she marched. The attorney for the DOE was visibly annoyed, excused herself, and ran after this person. There was a loud exchange outside in the corridor between the DOE attorney and the DOE representative who was scheduled to be the day's witness. Everyone heard their heated exchange. Moments later, the DOE attorney and the representative from the school were back in the hearing office glaring angrily at one another.

The hearing officer then announced, "We will now go on the record." The court reporter put on his headphones and pushed a button on the tape machine. The hearing officer read a required formal introduction. The hearing officer was halfway through this speech when the court reporter started waving his arms and shouted, "STOP! The recording machine is broken." The court reporter left the room telling everyone he needed to find a replacement machine, and that this could take at least a half hour, if not more. The CSE representative from the school stood up and yelled at the DOE lawyer, "I'm leaving because I have more important things to do than sit at a hearing that should not be going forward!" The hearing officer looked almost as shocked as the parents.

After this outburst, the parents' attorney asked the DOE attorney if they could speak outside of the hearing room. The attorney whispered to the parents that in light of what just occurred, and what the DOE representative said in front of the hearing officer, she was going to see if there was any chance of settling. While this discussion in the hallway was going on the parents remained in the hearing room with the hearing officer making small talk about the new Second Avenue subway and the weather. The two attorneys returned, and the parents' attorney asked to meet with the parents outside the hearing room. She informed them that the DOE attorney told her that she was not permitted to settle the case, and that she had no choice but to go forward. There was no explanation for the word "permitted."

It was 12:30 pm when the hearing finally began. The hearing officer once again gave her formal opening statement, followed by everyone in the room (with the exception of the court reporter), introducing him or herself. Next, the hearing officer stamped and marked each piece of evidence with an identifying number or letter, and read into the record what each piece of evidence was. Ten minutes into the start of this process, the attorney for the DOE asked to go off the record and excused herself to use the restroom, taking her cell phone with her. Once the DOE attorney returned and before going back on the record, the hearing officer asked how many witnesses each of the parties planned on presenting. The DOE attorney announced two—the representative from the CSE (the woman who was at the hearing and had stomped out), and someone from the proposed school. The parents' attorney asked which proposed school program and was told it would be someone from the second school with the 12:1:1 class.

The witness was not the Assistant Principal who the parent met on her school visit. Instead the DOE would present testimony from the teacher of the proposed 12:1:1 class. When hearing this, the parents' attorney asked that the hearing officer issue a subpoena for the Assistant Principal. The DOE attorney claimed that this Assistant Principal no longer worked at that school and had been assigned to another school in another district. The DOE attorney objected to the issuance of the subpoena. For the next 15 minutes a legal battle ensued between the two attorneys. The hearing officer cut this battle off, and in a stern tone told the DOE attorney that unless she agreed to produce this person as a witness she would issue a subpoena. If this person did not appear, the hearing officer would draw a negative inference about the appropriateness of the placement and give full credibility to the parent's testimony about the proposed class. Clearly the hearing officer had read the hearing request. The parents were not quite sure that they fully understood what was going on, but their attorney gave them a wink of assurance. The DOE attorney again excused herself, this time to call her supervisor.

This disappearance lasted twenty minutes and, by now, everyone's stomach was rumbling. Water bottles, rolls of mints, and granola bars emerged from briefcases and handbags, and there was small talk about current events. The DOE attorney returned and announced that she had located this Assistant Principal and there was no need to issue a subpoena. This person would voluntarily come as a witness. It was now close to 1:30 p.m. and only one piece of evidence had been submitted, out of a large stack. The judge turned to the parents' attorney, who informed her that the parents anticipated having seven witnesses for their case.

Before she was able to announce who these witnesses were, the DOE attorney screamed, "Seven witnesses, we'll never get this hearing over with." The hearing officer told her that this was the parents' request for a hearing and if the parents chose to have 27 witnesses, she would permit it. The hearing officer firmly told the DOE attorney to refrain from making comments and having outbursts.

The parents' seven witnesses would include: Dr. S., the neuropsychologist who evaluated Sophie; Ms. K, the educational consultant who visited the proposed school with the parents as well as observing Sophie at Churchill; Sophie's former speech therapist from the CPSE, who attended the initial CSE review; the Director of her former preschool, who was also at the CSE review; the admissions director of Churchill; Sophie's current kindergarten teacher at Churchill; and Sophie's mother. It was determined that they would need at least five more days for the hearing. It then took over half an hour for the attorneys and hearing officer to coordinate their schedules and come up with five days that worked for everyone. At 2:00 p.m. the dates were finally set.

TIP

In most NYC hearings, the scheduled hearing dates are not consecutive and there can be weeks or months between hearing dates. The average length of a tuition reimbursement hearing is between two and three days.

One more time, the hearing officer asked to go back on the record and stated, "After a lengthy discussion between the parties, it was determined that the DOE will present three witnesses and the parents will present seven. Five additional days of hearing have been scheduled, the first of which will start next week." The hearing officer stood up, wished everyone a good day, and was out the door.

This characterization is not a joke or spoof. It is based on an actual hearing. Attorneys practicing in this area who are reading this book will be laughing out loud, recognizing how many times they have been in similar situations.

On the next day of hearing, there was the usual delay in getting a room and court reporter, but the hearing was able to actually begin. It took almost an hour to enter all of the documents, which are referred to as evidence. Each document was an "exhibit." Parent exhibits were assigned a letter and DOE exhibits were given a number. Every piece of paper was counted, stamped, numbered, and read into the record by the hearing officer. Since the DOE had the burden of proof on prong one, the hearing officer asked the DOE attorney to begin with her opening statement followed by the parents statement.

The opening statement by the DOE attorney was short. She reiterated several times that the DOE had made FAPE available but that the parents never intended to use a public school placement as they had already signed a contract with Churchill prior to the Turning Five Review Meeting. The "aha" moment occurred, and the parents and their attorney finally understood why the DOE was fighting this case and refused to settle. The case was based solely on the issue of the date of contract (prong 3 of the Burlington/Carter test).

The opening statement made by Sophie's attorney presented the facts, stressing that the parents were open to all public school options. The attorney mentioned that Sophie's brother attended their local home-zoned school and that her parents had genuinely hoped that the public school program would be appropriate for Sophie too. Her parents had indeed visited the public school before even visiting Churchill School. She reiterated that the recommended second placement of the 12:1:1 class was made without a CSE review, without any new material, and without any participation of her parents or teachers. The parents' attorney forcefully argued that point claiming that this fact, in and of itself, rendered the placement invalid and a nullity.

After the opening statements, the parents' attorney asked that a subpoena be issued for the placement officer who sent out both final notices. Again the DOE attorney objected. The hearing officer agreed with the issuance of the subpoena, which was prepared by the parents' attorney and signed by the hearing officer.

The weeks and months rolled on and the hearing continued. After each day of hearing, the attorney was sent a transcript of the proceeding, which was based upon the recording taken by the court reporter. The parents asked for a copy and were sent one as well.

TIP

Witnesses give what is called direct testimony by responding to questions asked by their attorney. The opposing attorney then has the right to cross-examine the witness to show inconsistencies in their statements which negatively affect the credibility of the witnesses. It is imperative that every witness be prepared by the attorney and that they fully discuss what could possibly occur on cross-examination.

Given the number of witnesses that were testifying at Sophie's Impartial Hearing, it was still going on well into March when the CSE convened to develop another IEP for the following school year. This new review was conducted at the Churchill School by representatives from District 2, Region 9. This is the region and district where the Churchill school is located. This time, the CSE review team agreed to defer Sophie's case to CBST for the following school year. The parents' attorney tried to admit this new IEP and recommendation at the next day of the Impartial Hearing in order to establish that the prior review team was incorrect. However, the DOE attorney objected to this and the hearing officer sustained (agreed) to the objection and did not allow next year's IEP into evidence.

Of course, even with the denial of the submission of this evidence, everyone in the hearing room heard the facts. We like to say you can't un-ring a bell! In Sophie's case, the IHO heard that the new CSE team recognized that she needed a Non-Public School placement.

TIP

When an objection is sustained it means that the hearing officer agrees with the attorney who raised the objection to the entering of either the evidence or testimony.

TIP

If an objection is raised while a witness is testifying, the witness must stop speaking until the hearing officer makes a determination whether to sustain (agree with) or overrule (deny) the objection. The attorney that raises the objection indicates why he or she is objecting to the testimony. The other attorney indicates why they believe the objection is incorrect.

Sophie's mother was the last witness to testify. By the time she gave testimony she knew the issues perfectly well. Before testifying at the hearing, she once again met with her attorney to discuss the date they signed the contract. Sophie's mother was clear that she was at all times open to a public school placement. In fact, she visited her local public school well before signing any contract or even submitting an application to Churchill. She visited the public school at the same time she applied to private schools. Her plan was to keep all options open. The reason the parents signed a contract with Churchill was to hold a spot open for Sophie in the event there was no appropriate public school program. If Sophie was offered an appropriate public school placement and she accepted this, the terms of the Churchill contract permitted her to be released and all they would forfeit was their non-refundable deposit.

By the end of the hearing, the parents felt cautiously optimistic. They now understood that, while somewhat informal, an Impartial Hearing is litigation and there's always a chance of losing. What is equally worrying to the parents is that even if they won at the hearing, The DOE could choose to appeal to the New York State Education Department. They discussed this many times with their attorney who did not think that the DOE would appeal, particularly in light of the new deferral to CBST recommendation made by the CSE which could be submitted as evidence in such an appeal.

On the last day of hearing, the hearing officer ordered that in lieu of closing statements each attorney would submit a written Memorandum of Law. Both parties were given three weeks from the close of the hearing to submit the legal memoranda (one week to allow for the transcripts to arrive and two weeks to write the actual Memorandum). The IHO wished everyone well and walked out of the room.

All Impartial Hearing decisions must be in writing. A hearing officer will never issue an oral decision at the end of a hearing. The only instance when a parent knows the ruling during the hearing is if the parents and the DOE agree and the terms of the agreement are read into the record. This is referred to as "memorializing the terms of agreement," or a "settlement on the record."

A Memorandum of Law is sometimes referred to as a "legal brief." It is a written document citing and summarizing case law and then applying the law to the facts of the case in support of the party's position.

In Sophie's case, both parties submitted their Memorandum of Law on time, with no requests for extensions. Once this was done, all they could do was wait. They were far more relaxed because Sophie's deferral to CBST was officially approved and her placement at Churchill would be funded for the following year.

Precisely one month from the date that the memoranda were submitted, the parents received the hearing officer's written decision—the parents won! The decision was well-written and thorough. The parents' attorney doubted that the DOE would appeal, but she knew that she could not be one hundred percent certain for 35 days.

The Decision
A hearing officer must submit a written decision 30 days after the close of the hearing record. When briefs, or Memoranda of Law, are

requested, the record does not close until the date the briefs are received. The quality of the written decision varies. Some hearing officers write well-reasoned, well-thought-out decisions, while others do not. A well-written and well-reasoned decision is when the hearing officer makes determinations about the credibility of the witnesses and addresses all the issues. This type of decision is less likely to be appealed by the losing party. With the written decision comes a packet which describes the process by which the losing party can appeal the decision to the next administrative level.

> TIP
> _____
> *Although there is a 30-day requirement to issue a decision, many hearing officers request an adjournment or even multiple adjournments extending their time. These adjournments are generally granted.*

How a Hearing Decision Creates Pendency

A decision by an IHO that is not appealed creates what is known as **pendency on a decision**. In Sophie's case, had her placement for the next school year not been deferred to CBST for private school, pendency from the Impartial Hearing decision would have been extremely helpful and an important tool for the following years. Creating pendency on a decision means that because the hearing officer made a determination that Churchill was the appropriate placement for Sophie, and the DOE did not appeal or seek to overturn this determination, it becomes Sophie's "last-agreed-to placement" or her "Stay Put placement." Therefore, if in a subsequent school year the CSE makes a different determination about where she should go to school, her parent could file for a new hearing, and on the first day of the hearing invoke pendency to have Sophie "Stay Put" at Churchill until the conclusion of the new hearing, as well as for any subsequent appeals. This could stretch on for several years.

> TIP
> _____
> *No parent wants to be in the situation of having to fight year in and year out for a placement for their child. But when a parent takes the risk of private school placement, they open themselves up to this possibility.*

Payment

In Sophie's scenario, the DOE did not appeal and her parents were reimbursed the entire tuition upon proof of payment and attendance. The reimbursement check was remitted to their attorney's escrow account and then issued to the parents. The DOE has an office assigned solely for the purpose of processing payments as a result of Impartial

Hearing decisions. Parents are required to produce proof of payment in order to be reimbursed. This office works faster than the multistep process involved in reimbursement from settlement.

Legal Fees

If a parent prevails at an Impartial Hearing there is a provision in the IDEA that permits for the recoupment of their legal fees. The DOE does not make the recoupment process easy. There are forms and detailed time sheets that must be submitted and this is before the negotiations even begin. The DOE does not necessarily reimburse the full amount of legal fees. They try and cut both the hourly rate and the number of hours that have actually been spent. This often means there can be a shortfall between the time spent and billed and the time reimbursed.

If a parent uses an advocate instead of a lawyer to represent them at a hearing, they are not entitled to reimbursement of their legal fees. The provision of recouping legal fees applies only to an attorney. If a parent is an attorney and represents their own child, they are not permitted recoupment of fees for their representation. The fees for expert witnesses or private evaluations are not automatically eligible for reimbursement.

TIP
Every attorney or law firm has their own retainer and fee arrangement. You must discuss this with your attorney; do not be embarrassed. All attorneys understand a client's concern about fees and are comfortable discussing this.

Appeal

For all disputes arising under the IDEA, New York State operates under what is referred to as a "two-tier system of review." This means that before a parent or a school district can bring a case into federal (or state) court, they must go through an Impartial Hearing. If the matter is not resolved at the Impartial Hearing, then an appeal may be taken by the losing party to the New York State Education Department Office of State Review. An appeal is neither required nor is it automatic. The losing party at an Impartial Hearing has the right to take an appeal if they so choose.

An appeal to the SRO is begun by the filing of papers and forms. There are several review officers who are randomly assigned to a case. The SRO decides the appeal based on the "record" created at the actual hearing, which consists of the documents (exhibits) that were submitted to the hearing officer and the transcript of witness testimony. There are no physical appearances required or permitted in an SRO appeal. This means that no witnesses are called to give additional testimony and no lawyers give oral arguments.

There are strict requirements as to how to initiate an Appeal. These can be found at: *www.sro.nysed.gov/filing.html*.

> **TIP**
>
> *If a parent or school district does not follow the strict timeline required in filing an appeal, the appeal will be dismissed, and they will lose their right to seek review. Watch these deadlines.*

The party bringing the appeal is referred to as the *Petitioner* and the party responding or answering the appeal is referred to as the *Respondent*. At the time of the writing of this book, and for the last decade, the SRO has ruled in favor of school districts in the overwhelming majority of cases. We estimate that this is around 80 percent. This means that if a parent wins at an Impartial Hearing and a school district appeals, in over 80 percent of the cases the SRO sustains the appeal (agrees with the school district) and overturns the decision of the IHO. Similarly, if a school district wins and a parent appeals, in approximately 80 percent of the cases the SRO affirms (agrees with) the decision of the IHO in favor of the school district and dismisses the appeal. This is not good news for a parent.

> **TIP**
>
> *The DOE does not appeal every case it loses. In fact, the majority of the cases lost by the DOE at an Impartial Hearing are not appealed.*

> **TIP**
>
> *Don't panic! As in all areas of law, most cases settle. Have a strong underlying case, a good lawyer and good experts, and march on through the storm!*

> **TIP**
>
> *Settlement can occur at any point in the appeal process. Your lawyer should approach the DOE and maintain an open line of communication following the service of appeal papers.*

A decision rendered by the State Review Officer is binding *unless* the party who loses appeals in a Federal District Court. Technically, the second appeal can go into either Federal District Court or into State Supreme Court. Attorneys practicing in this area of law will invariably choose to go into Federal District Court. The federal courts tend to be more familiar with IDEA cases. State courts tend to be extremely deferential to decisions made by any State agency.

In New York State, there are four Federal District courts: Eastern, Northern, Southern and Western. New York City cases are heard in the

Southern or Eastern District. The party that loses at the SRO and chooses to bring a federal district court appeal has 90 days to file their Notice of Appeal. In federal court, the party that brings the appeal is referred to as the *Appellant* or *Plaintiff* and the party that responds to the appeal is the *Appellee* or *Defendant*. In this appeal, there is an opportunity for oral arguments by the attorneys and there can be additional testimony or witnesses at the discretion of the judge. There are court fees involved in the filing of this appeal. There is no set time frame for when this court renders a decision, and it is not unusual for this appeal to take several years.

The next level in the federal appeal process is the United States Court of Appeals for the Second Circuit. There are 13 judicial circuits throughout the USA. The Second Circuit is comprised of New York State, Vermont, and Connecticut. These 13 Courts of Appeal are considered to be among the most powerful and influential courts in the country. These courts not only set legal precedents, but they directly influence U.S. law. Everyone has the right to be heard in this court, but only after the district court renders a decision.

At this level of appeal, there are complex papers that must be filed in a timely manner, oral arguments, and new Memoranda of Law. These papers must be written and bound in a prescribed manner and this is very costly and time consuming. There are additional court fees involved as well. Any lawyer appearing before a Circuit Court panel of judges should be an expert in their area of law. It can take years from the time of the filing of the Second Circuit appeal papers before the case actually gets heard and decided. The decision rendered by the Circuit Court ends the process of the guaranteed right to appeal to a higher court.

At this juncture in the special education legal arena and process, the parties have had their case decided by an impartial hearing officer (IHO), the Office of State Review (SRO), a Federal District Court, and the Federal Circuit Court of Appeals. There is one additional, but remote, possibility for appealing. The losing party can attempt an appeal to the United States Supreme Court, the highest court in our country. There is no automatic right to have a case heard by the Supreme Court. The U.S. Supreme Court has complete and absolute discretion as to what cases they will hear. Out of the roughly 10,000 cases a year that file applications requesting the Supreme Court exercise its review powers, less than 100 cases are granted "certiorari," which is the right of review. When the Supreme Court grants certiorari and is willing to hear and decide a case it means that there is either a novel legal issue or the Circuit Courts throughout the country are split on an interpretation of a law.

CHAPTER SIX

Private Evaluations

To understand the importance of a private evaluation, let's talk about Jack, Sophie, and Lucy. These three children are all born in calendar year 2011 and have some type of developmental or learning delay. By the age of three, each child qualified for classification as a preschooler with a disability and received services from the CPSE. By the spring of 2016, each child was automatically referred to the school-age unit of the CSE for a turning-five review. If they are eligible to continue receiving special education or related services, the turning-five team will choose a specific classification, create an IEP, and make a program recommendation. The program for each child will begin in September 2016.

Sophie and Jack's parents believe that the kindergarten programs in their local public schools are not appropriate. Lucy's situation is different. Her parent is in the gray zone. Lucy could possibly succeed in an ICT class at the local public school which her parent desperately wants her to attend, but there is uncertainty.

Let's look at some additional and important facts concerning each child. Jack was born in December of 2011 and was two months premature and continued to display developmental delays. Sophie was born early in 2011, has a very high IQ, problems with attention, and is below age level in phonological processing and shows no interest in early reading skills. Sophie's father is dyslexic and there is a strong indication this is where she is headed. Then there's Lucy, our little girl in the gray zone, who was not identified as having problems until she was three years old and already in preschool. After a year and a half of CPSE services, Lucy's progress is remarkable. She is an extremely social child who is popular with her peers and is always invited for play dates and parties. Lucy's early academic skills are right where they are supposed to be.

In the fall of 2015, while each child is in their last year of preschool and receiving services through CPSE, their parents had a consultation. The first topic discussed was whether or not a private evaluation was needed. Jack's parents have reports from his developmental pediatrician, neurologist, speech, occupational, and physical therapists. In his case, every expert was of the opinion that Jack was not ready for kindergarten and recommended that he remain in his current preschool program for another year. For Jack, this would mean a continuation of his center and home-based program, under something that the attorney referred to as "preschool pendency." (See Chapter Four)

Sophie's parent toured private special education schools that were specifically for children with dyslexia and language-based learning disabilities and submitted applications to several of them. They are convinced that without the type of highly specialized instruction provided at these schools, Sophie will not be able to learn

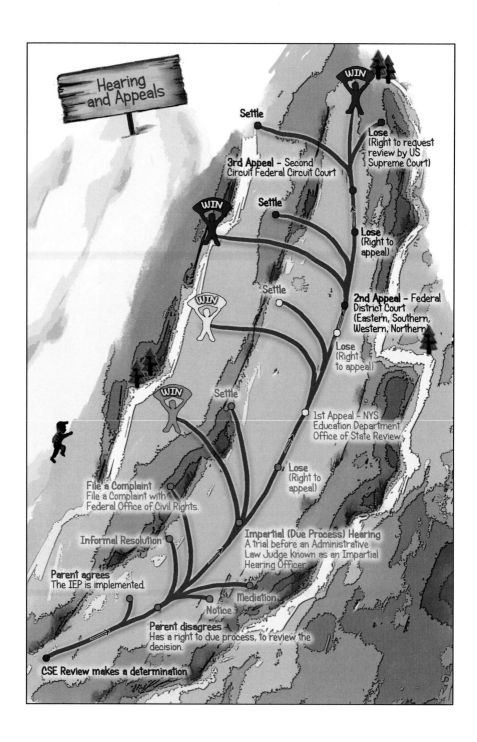

commensurate with her abilities or her peers. For Sophie's parent, the first choice is the Churchill School where she is a strong candidate. (See Chapter Three)

Then there's Lucy's mother who is on the fence. Lucy's brother attends the local public school and does very well. Her mother is impressed with the school and decided to meet with the assistant principal in charge of special education to discuss Lucy's background and her current needs. At this meeting, Lucy's mother was assured that the school could address her needs in an ICT class. She was told that in addition to the ICT class, which had two full-time teachers, the school would provide Lucy with an additional daily period of SETSS in order to receive very small group instruction in language arts. Lucy's mother has serious financial constraints and even the cost of a lawyer would be a stretch.

For Jack and Sophie, there is no doubt that they need a private evaluation. Their parents' next step would be to find an evaluator that they are comfortable with and determine what type of evaluation is needed. Jack needs an evaluator who would synthesize the evaluations already done, observe him in his current preschool setting, and attempt to administer some type of cognitive and academic testing.

Sophie, our Churchill candidate, needs a private evaluation with an evaluator who can fulfill two purposes. Firstly, the evaluation would be used as part of the admission application to the private schools. If the results of the evaluation indicate Sophie's need for a small school with small-group, highly specialized instruction, this would be essential material to present to the turning-five CSE review team in order to convince them to defer her case to the Central Based Support Team (CBST). If Sophie's parent could not reach an agreement with the CSE and their case proceeded to an Impartial Hearing (See Chapter Five), the evaluation will become evidence, and the evaluator must be willing to testify.

Finally, there is Lucy, whose situation is not as clear as Jack or Sophie's. Lucy's preschool teachers and related service providers all believe that she would be fine in an ICT kindergarten class, especially since she would be receiving a period a day of very small instruction in reading. Her mother is eager to try this program and more than willing to accept it. In these circumstances, a private evaluation is not absolutely required.

> **TIP**
> _____
> *There are many parents reading this book who are not considering another year of preschool or a private special education school placement. These parents want to use the program offered at their local public schools. Not every turning-five child needs a private*

evaluation. There are instances where the time and expense of a
private evaluation are not warranted or could be postponed,
allowing a child more time to develop and mature.

Another example of when a private evaluation is not necessary is when a child has been accepted into the ASD NEST program, and this is what the parent wants. There is no need for additional testing to support a determination that everyone agrees to. In both examples, a parent is getting exactly what they want from their school district with no expectation of disagreement or a potential Impartial Hearing.

However, and I'm taking a big sigh..., in my experience as a parent and seasoned professional, I have learned that answers to the big questions of life, particularly those concerning a child, rarely present with absolute certainty or razor-sharp clarity. These big questions usually come with a "But...," or a "What if...," or an "I'm not sure...," or that creeping feeling of doubt. Because of the uncertainty factor, more often than not, I find myself recommending a private evaluation, or at least a consultation with an experienced evaluator.

The juncture in a child's life when they leave preschool and enter kindergarten is a critical time for future development. The more information a parent has about their child, the clearer they will be in making an informed decision and in planning for the future. If, as an infant or toddler, a child was identified as having a developmental delay, it is highly unlikely that all of the problems and issues associated with this delay are fully resolved by the time the child is or approaches the age of five. For many children there will be persistent and obvious problems, while for other children the problems will be subtle, with residual or potential issues looming in the background.

There are risks and benefits in every choice and making a decision is difficult. When I help a parent sort through their questions and concerns the first two questions I ask are: *What program would be in the best interest of this child? What does this child need in order to maximize his or her potential?* In order to answer these questions, I carefully listen to a parent's description of their child and then turn to the independent evaluations and reports done by competent professionals. In some instances, the value of a private evaluation is simply to clarify or confirm a parent's opinion.

TIP
_____

It is critically important to remember that the standard of what is
in the best interest of your child is <u>*not*</u> *the legal standard that a*
school district is obligated to follow. A school district does not
have to consider or provide what is in a child's best interest or
what would maximize his or her potential. All that a school

district has to do is offer an education that is "merely appropriate".
Therefore, whenever you meet with anyone from the CSE/DOE
only ask for an "appropriate program" for your child—never
mention the term "best interest" and never ask for the "best
program."

Ideally, in order to confirm (or reject) the opinions of Jack, Sophie, and Lucy's parents, each child would be evaluated by an independent private professional who not only has skills and expertise in testing young children, but also has broad knowledge about the types of public and private school programs available within New York City.

> ### TIP
> *If the evaluator you are considering has never visited an ICT*
> *program in a NYC public school and this is an option that you are*
> *considering or one that your school district might recommend, my*
> *advice is to change evaluators! A good evaluator will also guide*
> *parents to good public and private programs. Do not use evalua-*
> *tors whose practice is located outside of NYC. Remember, the*
> *NYC DOE is a world unto itself.*

A parent usually goes to attorneys to understand their options, legal rights, and to place themselves in the best possible position to achieve the ultimate outcome that they want. Parents who are seeking another year of preschool or who are contemplating placing their child in a private special education school, must remember that these options could involve litigation (an Impartial Hearing or even an appeal).

> ### TIP
> *All Impartial Hearings are won and lost by expert witnesses. Your*
> *opinion about what your child needs will be listened to but at a*
> *hearing it is rarely (if ever) enough to convince a hearing officer or*
> *to win your case. In order for you to be best positioned for a*
> *positive outcome at an Impartial Hearing, the expert opinion of a*
> *competent evaluator is essential.*

Even Lucy's mother who is planning on using the public school and is not anticipating being at an Impartial Hearing, would be wise to have a private evaluation, if affordable. For Lucy, the choice of an ICT public school placement, even with SETSS, comes with what I refer to as "watchful waiting." This means that her parent would need to actively monitor Lucy's progress in this program. The best way to monitor progress is to have an objective baseline of academic skills as assessed by a private evaluator. This type of baseline evaluation is an insurance policy. What if the ICT class size is too large and Lucy is not keeping up with her peers regardless of the support and help provided at school and at home? If this occurs, her parent would need to look for alternative programs, which most likely would include a private special education school. At that point a private evaluation is strongly recommended.

Frequently Asked and Important Questions About Private Evaluations

What is a private evaluation?

When professionals in the field of special education refer to a "private evaluation" they generally mean a Psychoeducational (**Psychoed**) Evaluation or Neuropsychological (**Neuropsych**) Evaluation. However, in actuality a private evaluation is not limited to these two types of evaluations and can include other disciplines such as: audiology (including evaluating hearing), developmental pediatrics, neurology, occupational therapy, physical therapy, speech and language pathology (including evaluating central auditory processing), or psychiatry.

What is the difference between a school psychologist, a clinical psychologist, and a neuropsychologist?

The function of a **school psychologist** is to enhance the development of children in educational settings. This type of psychologist generally works in a school or school systems. Their job includes conducting psychoeducational assessments and providing counseling or consultation to classroom teachers and other school staff. The qualifications of a school psychologist are a 60-credit master's degree, an academic one-year internship, and passing a state certification examination. A school psychologist is not required to hold a doctoral degree, although there are some school psychologists who do have this advanced degree. It is the school psychologist that often provides in-school counseling to children identified as needing this related service.

A **clinical psychologist** is a doctoral-level professional who can work in a school, hospital, community health center, or private practice. In addition to holding a Ph.D. or Psy.D. degree in psychology, this type of psychologist must also complete a practicum, write and defend a doctoral dissertation, finish a one-year residency, and pass a licensing examination. Clinical psychologists evaluate and assess children and adults as well as provide therapy and counseling. The type of psychoeducational evaluation conducted by a clinical psychologist goes into greater detail and depth than one done by a school psychologist in a school setting.

A **neuropsychologist**, like a clinical psychologist, must hold a doctoral degree, complete a practicum, write and defend a dissertation, complete a residency, and pass a licensing examination. In addition to these criteria, a neuropsychologist must also complete two years of post-doctoral training. When conducting their evaluations, a neuropsychologist applies principles based upon the scientific study of human behavior as it relates to normal and abnormal functioning of the brain and central nervous system. A neuropsychologist can work in the same settings as a clinical psychologist and perform the same tasks. A neuropsychologist administers not only the same types of tests that a school or clinical psychologist does, but usually does more advanced testing in areas of attention, language, memory, emotional, sensory processing, and other areas of functioning.

> TIP
> _____
> *I strongly advise against using a master's-degree-level psychologist when doing a private evaluation. Regardless of this person's years of experience, or your feelings of affection toward this evaluator, a doctoral degree should be the minimum qualification of any private psychologist conducting an evaluation.*

A private evaluation, with an experienced doctorate-level evaluator, provides parents with a comprehensive, objective, and highly professional understanding of their child's cognitive functioning, academic achievement, learning styles, learning differences or delays, emotional functioning, attention issues, as well as what the best and most appropriate educational program is for their child.

What is the difference between a psychoeducational evaluation and a neuropsychological evaluation?

A **psychoed evaluation** can be administered by a school psychologist, clinical psychologist, or neuropsychologist. A **neuropsych evaluation** can only be administered by a certified neuropsychologist. Both types of evaluations share several common features; these include a social history provided by the parent, as well as cognitive and academic testing of the child. An experienced clinical psychologist will also include an evaluation of attention, a social and emotional assessment, and personality functioning. A neuropsych evaluation includes all of these features as well as an evaluation of a child's expressive, receptive, and pragmatic language, executive functioning, memory, learning styles, and visual spatial abilities. Since a neuropsychologist is trained to do both types of evaluations they will often determine which is needed.

> TIP
> _____
> *A child who has more complex medical conditions such as cancer, neurological-related conditions, and/or physical disabilities,*

should have an evaluation with a professional with experience
working with these types of medical issues.

What types of tests are generally done?

A test of a child's intelligence or cognitive functioning is commonly referred to as an IQ test. For very young children under the age of six, either a WPPSI-IV or a Stanford Binet V is the instrument typically used to measure intelligence. For children between the ages of six to sixteen, the most common test is the Wechsler Intelligence Scaled for Children, Fifth Edition (WISC V). There are other tests of intelligence, but the ones mentioned above are the most popular.

Since the WISC V and the WPPSI are language-based tests, when a child has severe language delays there are other tests used to measure nonverbal intelligence. Again, a skilled clinical psychologist or neuro-psychologist will have familiarity with these measures. Two popular tests measuring non-verbal intelligence that I have seen used are the Leiter and C Toni. Some psychologists administer abridged IQ tests, but clearly these are not as accurate as they only offer verbal and nonverbal screening measures and exclude measures of processing speed and working memory. These abridged tests are generally done by school psychologists within school settings.

Assessing a child's academic achievement generally includes a battery of testing in the areas of reading, writing, and mathematics. Some of the more common academic achievement tests are: Woodcock Johnson Tests of Achievement - Third Edition, referred to as the WJ III; the Wechsler Individual Achievement Test - Third Edition, referred to as the WIAT; or the Kaufman Test of Educational Achievement, referred to as the KTEA.

When a clinical psychologist or a neuropsychologist conducts an evaluation, it can also include assessments of a child's emotional and behavioral functioning and other cognitive processes involved in learning, such as attention.

A classroom observation is an important aspect of a private evaluation. Be sure to ask any private evaluator that you choose if he or she is willing to do a classroom observation as part of their assessment. It is not required, but I find it helpful in educational planning and it becomes extremely important if your case should proceed to an Impartial Hearing. At the very least, the evaluator must speak with the child's preschool teachers and/or SEIT.

TIP
_____

If the DOE does not do a classroom observation as part of their
turning-five assessment, the fact that your private evaluator has
done one could be a very important factor if disputing a placement.

TIP
_____

School districts outside of NYC often use two different profession-als to do a psychoed assessment: A psychologist (to administer the intelligence or IQ portion of the evaluation) and an educational evaluator or classroom teacher (to administer the educational assessments). This split approach is hardly ever used by the NYC DOE, which prefers to have the school psychologist do both parts of the evaluation. When doing a private evaluation, I do not recommend this split approach.

What type of evaluation will the DOE provide?

All school districts will provide, free of charge, a psychoed evalua-tion once every three years or when this is reasonably requested by a parent. School districts do a basic psychoed evaluation, which includes an IQ and academic testing. The quality of these evaluations varies greatly and depends on who the evaluator is. A parent cannot choose a specific evaluator, and is limited by who the school or CSE assigns.

A DOE evaluation is done by a licensed, certified school psycholo-gist, who can either hold a master's or doctoral degree, and must hold New York State certification. A DOE psychoed is generally done in one testing session lasting about two hours. There is no advanced interview with the parent by the psychologist, and there is no feedback session when the testing is complete. The testing can occur either during school hours or after school. The test does not take into consideration that a child can be fatigued, disinterested, or scared of the evaluator. The location of the testing is either at the home-zoned public school or at the CSE offices. There is no opportunity for a child to establish a trusting relationship with this stranger. The physical setting can be frightening and the circumstances surrounding the administration of the evaluation are often not ideal for motivating a child. These factors can sometimes give rise to inaccurate results.

In contrast to the psychoed done by the DOE, a private evaluation occurs over multiple days and sessions, allowing time for the child to develop a trusting and working relationship with the evaluator. Private evaluations generally permit frequent breaks and rewards for a child's effort. A private evaluation always provides a parent with an in-depth feedback session and permits parents to preview reports prior to finaliz-ing them. A private evaluator does not have any agenda other than what is best for the child and family. A private evaluator is not employed by anyone other than the parent, and they do not have to take into account the policies or position of a school district.

TIP

The DOE generally does not do a psychoed evaluation for a turning -five student. Therefore, having a private evaluation lends greater credibility to your position at any possible hearing or dispute.

The evaluations done by the CSE in New York City do not compare with a comprehensive and thorough private evaluation. The old adage "you get what you pay for" absolutely applies. Keep in mind that there are exceptions, and I have seen some fine evaluations done by public school psychologists. There are even some doctoral level school psychologists who have training in neuropsychology. These reports are good, but they are few and far between.

TIP

Always keep in mind that an evaluator from a school district does not work for you. These professionals are employees of the school district and are obliged to follow directives issued by their employer. You will not get a chance to preview the report generated from the evaluation, and you will not have an opportunity for an in-depth conversation with the evaluator prior to the issuance of the report.

It is not necessary to have a private evaluation every year; however, there are important times in a child's development that warrant this type of thorough private evaluation or re-evaluation.

How to choose a private evaluator?

New York City is the world capital of special education. Our city's private schools and programs are in a stellar league of their own. There are scores of competent, highly qualified, and excellent evaluators and therapists. The answer to the question of who to use as an evaluator is very subjective. In choosing a psychologist to evaluate your child, it is imperative that this person has experience with special needs children, particularly young children, as well as being familiar with the private and public special education schools and programs in NYC. I cannot underscore this enough. It is not helpful to use someone in another state because they are a family friend and will do it for free. This evaluator might be called upon to testify at a CSE review or an Impartial Hearing. If this person does not have firsthand knowledge about NYC public and private schools, their testimony will have limited value.

TIP

If you are considering private school placement for your child, call the director of admissions at the private school and ask for their "short list" of private psychologists. Also ask whether they prefer a neuropsych or psychoed. Also ask if there is any specific type of testing that the school requires. Some private schools require what is known as projective testing. This is testing that assesses a child's emotional functioning. Another important question to ask is when the private school recommends having the child evaluated. Usually evaluations are done in the early fall preceding the year that the child would attend the school.

The most important consideration in choosing a private evaluator is driven by the human factor. In simplest terms, do you like and trust this person? Are you comfortable with this person being with your child for hours and days? Is this person someone who you think your child can relate to? Is this person someone you can cry with if you need to? Like any other important relationship in your life, is there person-to-person chemistry?

Once you get past the human factors, here are some additional considerations:

- Is the person accessible? Will he or she answer your emails and return your phone calls? How easy was it to make an initial appointment?
- How soon after the evaluation is completed can you expect a written report? School applications have deadlines. Be sure that you have your report well in advance of any deadline.
- Is the evaluator familiar with the private special education schools as well as the mainstream public and private schools? Specifically ask the person when was the last time that they visited the schools you are considering.
- Will the evaluation include a classroom observation?
- Does this evaluator have a professional network that they can refer you to if your child needs to see a neurologist, psychiatrist, speech therapist, OT, PT, behaviorist, or private tutor?
- Will the evaluator meet with you after the testing to discuss results and make specific recommendations?
- Is this evaluator on the list of recommended evaluators from the private schools you are considering?
- Will this evaluator permit you to review a draft of the report before it is finalized to assure the factual accuracy?
- Is this person willing to testify at an Impartial Hearing? Does your attorney know this person?

Once you have a private evaluation, what should you do with it?

The final copy of a child's evaluation has several purposes. Most importantly, it provides a parent with objective data to assess the child's level of functioning, the issues the child is struggling with, and what type of learning environment the child needs in order to succeed. If a parent is applying to private special education schools (either Approved or Independent), the private evaluation should accompany the application. The report is a major component in a private school's determination of whether a child is an appropriate candidate for the school.

If a child will be attending a public school, the evaluation report still serves an important function in helping the classroom teacher understand the child, as well as to monitor a child's progress. The report should be given to the teachers and public school administrators at the start of the school year.

TIP

A private evaluation should be shared with the turning-five review team, but if you are planning on pendency or a private school this must be discussed with your attorney first.

TIP

There can only be one version of any report. I am sometimes asked by a parent if it is permissible to have one version of an evaluation for private school applications and one version for the CSE. The answer is ABSOLUTELY NOT! It is permissible to have updates done after the first evaluation with new data and new recommendations, but there can never ever be an A version and a B version of the same evaluation.

TIP

Even if you have submitted your private evaluation prior to the actual Turning Five Review Meeting, bring at least one extra copy with you to the actual meeting.

Is there a way to get a private evaluation paid for by the DOE?

If a parent is not satisfied with the evaluation done by the DOE and wants an independent evaluation at public expense, the parent must write to the district, indicate the specific reasons why they disagree with the DOE evaluation, and then ask for an independent evaluation at public expense. Remember, this means that there has been a school district evaluation that the parent disagrees with. This disagreement can be the way in which the test was administered, the failure of the evaluation to test the child in all areas, or the belief that the findings of the evaluation were not reflective of the child.

Once a parent submits their written request (sent certified mail return receipt) for an independent evaluation at school district expense, the school district must respond within a relatively short period of time, by either agreeing to the request and arranging for a contract agency to evaluate the child, or by taking the parent to an Impartial Hearing seeking a determination from an impartial hearing officer as to whether or not an independent evaluation is warranted. This is one of the few instances where the DOE can actually request an Impartial Hearing against a parent. There is no specific definition of what a relatively short period of time is. Generally, we consider two weeks to be a reasonable period of time.

If the DOE agrees to pay for an independent evaluation, they will send the parent an "Assessment Authorization" form which allows the parent to find an evaluator at the rate set by the DOE. This does not mean that the evaluator who the parent wants is willing to accept the DOE rate. If a parent does not follow these procedures and obtains the private evaluation before getting the DOE's approval, they cannot back into a request for reimbursement. If you find an evaluator willing to take the Assessment Authorization, the final report that is prepared "belongs" to the DOE. Generally, a parent is not given a draft preview of the report. Also, this report becomes part of your child's records. (This is all very different for children living outside of New York City.)

TIP
There are instances where a parent has not followed these procedures but can still have their private evaluation paid for by the DOE. This generally requires an Impartial Hearing.

TIP
There are circumstances where I recommend requesting an Independent Educational Evaluation (IEE) but this is done on a case-by-case basis. If possible, I always prefer a completely private evaluation with which a parent has ownership of the report and a completely private relationship with the evaluator.

What are the other types of private evaluations?

In addition to a psychoed or neuropsych evaluation, a private evaluation can also include: an Audiological Evaluation, a Central Auditory Processing Evaluation, an Evaluation by a Developmental Pediatrician, a Neurological Evaluation, an Occupational Therapy Evaluation, a Physical Therapy Evaluation, a Psychiatric Evaluation, or a Speech Therapy Evaluation.

Audiological Evaluation

An audiological assessment is performed by a credentialed and qualified audiologist who holds a current American Speech-Language-Hearing Association (ASHA) certificate of clinical competence and/or a valid state license if required by state law. An audiological assessment for a turning-five child would be recommended for a child who is at risk of, suspected of, or identified with an auditory impairment or disorder, or a hearing disability. The purpose of an audiological assessment is to determine the status of the auditory mechanism; identify the type, degree, and configuration of hearing loss for each ear; characterize associated disability and potentially handicapping conditions; assess the ability to use auditory information in a meaningful way (functional hearing); identify individual risk factors and the need for surveillance of late-onset or progressive hearing loss; assess candidacy for sensory devices (e.g., hearing aids, hearing assistive devices, cochlear implants); refer for additional evaluation and intervention services when indicated; provide counseling for families/caregivers regarding audiological assessment findings and recommendations; communicate findings and recommendations, with parental consent, to other professionals working with the child in order to consider the need for additional assessments and/or screenings.

Central Auditory Processing Evaluation

Central auditory processing refers to the way in which a child processes auditory information. Some children have normal or near-normal hearing, but still display characteristics of misinterpreting auditory information. This misinterpretation may be attributed to a deficit in the way in which the child processes auditory information. The purpose of the central auditory processing evaluation is to help define the specific auditory processing difficulties that a child is experiencing and to recommend appropriate remediation. Performance on auditory processing tests is measured according to chronological age expectancies.

Evaluation by a Developmental Pediatrician

A developmental pediatrician is a medical doctor who has completed a pediatric residency and has additional subspecialty training and certification within the field of developmental behavioral pediatrics. Board certification requires completion of a developmental behavioral fellowship, passing a national examination, followed by participating in a continuing medical education program. A developmental pediatrician focuses on a child's development, including assessing the child's gross and fine motor skills, language development, cognition, behavior, and learning. A developmental pediatrician uses a combined medical, neuropsychological, and neurodevelopmental approach in their assessment and evaluation. Such an evaluation would also consider heredity, medical history, current health status, neurologic evaluation, developmental evaluation, and assessment of specific areas of concern.

Neurological Evaluation

Neurologists are medical doctors with specialized training in diseases of the brain and nervous system. A child neurologist has specific training in pediatrics and pediatric neurology. They have expertise in attention disorders, learning difficulties, childhood epilepsy and seizures, congenital brain malformations, childhood stroke, and developmental and behavioral issues of infancy and childhood. A neurological exam is a simple series of tests that allows the neurologist to watch a child's nervous system in action and make assessments of their mental status (level of awareness and interaction with the environment), motor and sensory skills, balance, coordination, and reflexes. There are different components to a standard neurological exam and the ones that a neurologist will focus on depend on specific factors relating to the child's symptoms, age, and health.

Occupational Therapy Evaluation

Occupational Therapy (OT) is the assessment and treatment of physical and psychiatric conditions using specific purposeful activity to prevent disability and promote independent function in all aspects of a child's daily life. It is used with a child who has difficulties with the practical and social skills necessary for everyday life. Occupational therapists hold a license and certification after completing a course of study leading to a master's degree. They are responsible for determining the need for OT services, which is done through a comprehensive evaluation. The therapist may use screening, standardized, or non-standardized tests, depending on the need and type of information sought. Once a child is (or approaches) five years of age, the evaluation should be directly related to their ability to function and be successful in school.

There is no one particular assessment tool that the occupational therapist should or must use. The therapist should be familiar with a variety of methods to gather the necessary information and make an informed decision. An OT evaluation can be used to find out information about a child's **sensory processing skills**, which is the way the body takes in and processes information from the sensory systems of the body. An OT will specifically assess the child's **visual system** (how a child processes what he sees); **auditory system** (how a child processes what he hears); **tactile system** (how a child processes what he touches); and **vestibular system** (how a child processes himself in motion). In addition, occupational therapists may assess a child's **proprioceptive functioning** (how a child processes his actual movement); **motor planning** functioning (how a child can plan and make movements); self-regulation skills (how a child calms himself); **visual motor** and **visual perceptual skills**; handwriting skills; fine motor skills (such as cutting with scissors); upper extremity use; limb strength; range of motion; and bilateral coordination of the hands (ability to use both hands together).

Physical Therapy Evaluation

Physical Therapy (PT) improves a child's gross motor functioning and focuses on enhancing strength, balance, and coordination with gross motor movements. A physical therapist is a licensed certified professional who has completed a course of study leading to a doctoral degree. PTs work towards helping a child develop age-appropriate motor skills. PTs can retrain a child's brain on how to control motor movements. They can also recommend and fit a child for adaptive equipment such as orthotics, prosthetics, standers, walkers, canes, strollers, wheelchairs, specialized seating, and bath systems. A physical therapist may also use manual skills such as massaging, craniosacral therapy, joint mobilizations, and manual traction to decrease pain and spasms in the muscles.

A PT evaluation for a child is a one-on-one, play-based assessment with the child and caregivers. A child's muscle range of motion, strength, mobility, muscle tone, and gross motor skills are evaluated. This evaluation will be hands-on using a variety of tests to help establish a child's gross motor function.

Speech Therapy Evaluation

If a child requires support to develop speech and/or language skills, they are seen by a Speech-language pathologist (SLP), also known as a speech therapist. An SLP holds a master's degree, has passed a certification exam, and has worked under supervision for a number of years. A speech-language assessment or evaluation is a complex process. Assessing, describing, and interpreting a child's communication ability requires the integration of a variety of information gathered during the evaluation process. A speech-language pathologist will look at a child's understanding and use of language.

Language can be broken down into a number of categories: **Morphology** involves the structure of words, such as the root words combined with prefixes and suffixes, compound words, etc. **Syntax** involves the rules governing the order and combination of words in the formation of sentences, and the relationships among the elements within a sentence or between two or more sentences. **Semantics** is the system that patterns individual word meanings, and combining of word meanings, to form the content of a sentence. **Pragmatics** is the system that allows the speaker to use his/her communication skills in a variety of settings. In addition, the SLP will evaluate a child's ability to produce the speech sounds of the language. **Articulation** and **phonology** refers to your child's ability to hear and use the sound system of a language. If your child requires an oral peripheral evaluation, the speech language pathologist will look into the child's mouth to examine the articulators to ensure that the mechanism for speech production is intact.

Summary

To fully comprehend the value of private evaluations, it is important that parents understand the entire turning-five process. It is for this reason that I have placed this chapter at the end of the book, so readers first familiarize themselves with what options are available for their children and what has to be done to maximize the chance of success in achieving the desired outcome. I have purposely not included the names of specific evaluators since this list changes. When I meet a parent for a consultation, I have a list of twenty psychologists and neuropsychologists that I routinely refer to. Other lawyers and advocates practicing in this field should have a similar list. Parent chat rooms and places like the Jewish Community Center (JCC) on the Upper West Side of Manhattan are additional resources for parents. It is wise to start with a psychoed or neuropsych evaluation and then see if the child needs any additional evaluations. A psychologist who conducts the psychoed or neuropsych generally has lists of related service providers and evaluators that they work with and can refer parents to.

Learning the Language

This glossary is applicable to New York State. There are, however, some terms that are specific to New York City. These will be identified with an (*). If you are searching for a term that is more commonly known by its acronym (e.g., ABA, for Applied Behavioral Analysis), you will find it listed under its acronym.

12:1:1 (or 12:1:1 Classroom or 6:1:1 Classroom, etc.) - These ratio expressions refer to the ratio of students to teachers to paraprofessionals (paras) in a special education classroom. So, for example, a 12:1:1 Classroom has twelve students, one teacher, and one para.

12-MSY (12 Month School Year) - Also referred to as ESY (Extended School Year). Generally, a school year runs 10 months (September through June). However, there are children who require school or related services during the months of July and August, thus making their program a 12-month school year. The standard used in determining whether a child is eligible for a 12-month school year is if the child will have a *substantial regression* absent being in a 12-month program. This designation will appear in the child's IEP.

3-Prong Burlington/Carter Test - See **Three-Prong Burlington/Carter Test**

504 Plan - "504" refers to Section 504 of the Rehabilitation Act of 1973. This federal law specifies that no child with a disability can be excluded from participating in federally funded programs or activities (including school). A 504 Plan is used when a student's disability does not warrant an IEP (Individual Education Program), but the student still requires modifications and accommodations to attend. The plan specifically identifies, in writing, what types of modifications and accommodations are needed so that the student has opportunity to perform at the same level as his peers. This can include such things as wheelchair ramps, blood sugar monitoring, an extra set of textbooks, a peanut-free lunch environment, a tape recorder or keyboard for taking notes, testing accommodations, or even home instruction.

ABA (Applied Behavioral Analysis) - A behaviorally oriented methodology frequently used to educate children on the autism spectrum or who have significant behavioral issues. It is usually associated with the use of "discrete trials" and the recording of data about the child's behaviors or their mastery of the skills being taught.

Accommodation - An accommodation is a change that helps a student overcome or work around their disability. An example of an accommodation would be allowing a student who has trouble writing to give answers orally, or to use a computer.

Achievement Test - A test or series of tests that measure competency in a particular area of knowledge or skill set; these types of tests measure a student's mastery or acquisition of skills in that subject area.

ACT - The ACT® test assesses a high school student's general educational development and ability to complete college-level work.

ADA (Americans with Disabilities Act) - This federal act prohibits discrimination on the basis of disability in the areas of employment, public transportation, public accommodations, telecommunications, access to public services programs, and activities of state and local governments, as well as those of commercial facilities, private businesses, and nonprofit service providers. The ADA was signed into law on July 26, 1990.

Adaptive Behavior - This term is best thought of as "practical intelligence." It is usually measured on scales identifying how well a child (or adult) can manage within his or her own environment.

ADHD (Attention Deficit Hyperactivity Disorder) - A neurobiological condition resulting in either inattentive type of behaviors, difficulties focusing and/or concentrating, or impulsive behaviors; it is also commonly referred to as ADD.

*Advocates For Children of New York - This highly regarded nonprofit agency works on behalf of children who are at the greatest risk for school-based discrimination and/or academic failure due to poverty, disability, race, ethnicity, immigrant or English language learner status, homelessness, or involvement in the foster care or juvenile justice systems. This agency offers a wealth of information about special education law. *www.advocatesforchildren.org*

ADR (Alternative Dispute Resolution) - Methods used to settle disputes outside of court (trial) or Impartial Hearings. These can include: arbitration, mediation, negotiation and settlement.

Advocate - A non-attorney who assists a parent in obtaining appropriate accommodations, modifications, services, and programs from a school district for a child.

AE (Age Equivalency) - A term sometimes used to measure a child's level of academic or language functioning. It is equally common to measure scores by use of grade equivalents or percentiles.

AIT (Auditory Integration Training) - A program designed to address sensory problems such as hearing distortions and oversensitive hearing. It is believed that these hearing problems cause discomfort, interfere with attention, comprehension, and ability to learn in children diagnosed with learning disabilities as well as those on the autism spectrum. The NYS Department of Health recommends that AIT not be used to treat young children since it is considered an experimental procedure with very little empirical evidence supporting its efficacy.

ALJ (Administrative Law Judge) - The person who sits as a judge at a Due Process Impartial Hearing, also referred to as an impartial hearing officer (IHO). This judge takes and reads evidence, listens to opening and closing statements, hears witness testimony, and when the hearing is over, renders a written decision finding either in favor of the parent(s) or the school district.

Alternate Assessments - A method of assessing progress and need in a child when, due to the severity of their disability, they cannot participate in standardized testing. Typically, an alternate assessment can include oral reports, projects, portfolios or collections of work, demonstrations, performances, and experiments.

AMAC (Association in Manhattan for Autistic Children) - A New York State approved private special education school. (See Chapter Three)

Annual Goal - A required component of every child's IEP. Goals are considered to be a road map designed to guide the teacher and related service provider by directing them to work on specific academic, language, and social/emotional tasks. Goals should be specific to the needs of the child. They should be positive and describe a skill that can be taught and measured.

Annual Review - A student who has an IEP and receives special education and/or related services must have his/her IEP reviewed within one year of the date of the last IEP meeting. Parents and school staff should review the student's present levels of performance, determine whether last year's goals were met, and then create new goals. The Annual

Review also provides the opportunity to review and discuss the student's educational services/programs and goals, and to consider whether the student would benefit from placement in a different program.

AP (Assistant Principal) - Public schools usually have more than one assistant principal. Generally, one of these administrators is assigned to oversee the special education program in the school.

APE (Adaptive Physical Education) - Physical education, commonly referred to as gym, is a graduation requirement for all students. There are some children who, because of their physical disabilities, cannot complete this requirement without the formal gym program being adapted and modified to take into account the child's physical challenges.

API (Alternate Performance Indicators) - The educational goals against which the achievement of a student recommended for Alternate Assessment will be measured. These indicators must be appropriate to the student's abilities and needs.

Appeal - In the context of special education, the party who loses at an Impartial Hearing has an absolute right to an appeal. In New York State, the appeal by the losing party from the decision rendered by the impartial hearing officer (IHO) is filed with the New York State Education Department's Office of State Review (commonly known as the SRO). The party that loses at the State Review appeal has the right to yet another appeal, this time either in State Court via a proceeding under Article 78 or in Federal Court. (In special education matters, I always recommend appealing to Federal Court rather than State Court.)

Approved Non-Public School - A private special education school that is contracted by the New York State Education Department to provide educational services to students with disabilities who cannot be appropriately served by a public program. School districts have the ability to place students into these programs and fund them. The list of Approved Non-Public Schools is published on the New York State Education website: *www.p12.nysed.gov/specialed/privateschools*. Sometimes these schools are referred to as Non-Public Schools (NPS).

Apraxia - A neurological disorder of motor planning, characterized by the inability to execute or carry out learned purposeful movements despite having the desire and the physical ability to perform the movements.

Apraxia of Speech - Also referred to as Childhood Apraxia of Speech, is a motor speech disorder. For reasons not yet fully understood, children with apraxia of speech have great difficulty planning and producing the precise, highly refined, and specific series of movements of the tongue, lips, jaw, and palate that are necessary for intelligible speech. Apraxia of speech is sometimes called verbal apraxia, developmental apraxia of speech, or verbal dyspraxia. There is an organization known as the Childhood Apraxia of Speech Association of North America (CASANA), which serves as an outstanding reference site. *www.apraxia-kids.org*

Aptitude Test - A test used to measure a child's ability to learn in some particular area.

Arbitration - A formal hearing presided over by one or more arbitrators who may be officially sanctioned to reach decisions that are binding on the parties. Participation in this type of resolution is usually voluntary and it is used as an alternative to a formal court proceeding.

ARC - Also referred to as "The Arc." This is America's largest nonprofit organization supporting people with intellectual and other developmental disabilities and their families since 1949. *www.nysarc.org*

ARI (Autism Research Institute) - A nonprofit organization established in 1967 that promotes alternative treatments for autism. It conducts and sponsors research, networking, and education programs. *www.autism.com*

Article 4 of New York's Civil Practice Law and Rules - A State Court proceeding in which the court reviews the propriety of an administrative decision.

Article 17A - This refers to Article 17A of the Surrogate Court Procedure Act. At age 18 all people are considered to have reached majority and are technically free of their parents' decisions. In the case of a child with a disability, this is also true, and in order to have a parent or another person appointed to legally make decisions for this person, a guardian must be appointed. For a person with an intellectual or developmental disability, one way of doing this is through a guardianship petition in the Surrogate Court. This grants very general authority for the guardian. The process can be completed without an attorney. For more information about the process try calling (518) 388-2892 and speaking with the Director of the Protection and Advocacy for Persons with Developmental Disabilities (PADD) program. This person will answer questions and direct you to a PADD office, which may assist in training you for the application process for Article 17A.

Article 81 - This refers to Article 81 of New York's Mental Hygiene Law and is another court proceeding for the appointment of a guardian when a child turns 18 years old. This guardianship application is made in the State Supreme Court and generally requires the services of an attorney who is familiar with this statute. After an application is made, the court appoints a "court evaluator" to determine the limitations of the proposed ward (person needing a guardian). The Article 81 order may specify duties and limitations for the guardian. If granted, Article 81 authorizes a court to appoint a guardian to manage the personal and/or financial affairs of a person who cannot manage for himself or herself because of incapacity.

Article 89 - This refers to Article 89 of the New York Education Law: Children with Handicapping Conditions. This is New York's counterpart to the federal statue known as the IDEA. It is the basis in state law for most of the rights available to special education children/students.

Articulation - The movement of the tongue, lips, jaw, and other organs to make speech sounds, or simply the act of speech.

ASD (Autism Spectrum Disorder) - ASD typically appears during the first three years of life and affects a child's ability to communicate and interact with others. ASD is defined by a certain set of behaviors and is a "spectrum disorder" that affects individuals differently and to varying degrees. There is no known single cause for ASD, but it is believed to be a disorder of neural development characterized by impaired social interaction and communication and by restricted and repetitive behavior. ASD affects the way information is processed in the brain due to differences in how nerve cells and their synapses organize. Why this occurs is not well understood.

Although ASD varies significantly in character and severity, it occurs in all ethnic and socioeconomic groups and affects every age group. Up until the DSM-V, children could be diagnosed with subcategories on the autism spectrum: autistic disorder, Asperger's disorder, childhood disintegrative disorders, or PDD-NOS. With the advent of the DSM-V in May 2013, now only one diagnosis, ASD, is medically given. However, patients diagnosed with ASD may also be described in terms of any known genetic cause (e.g., Fragile X Syndrome or Rett Syndrome).

ASL (American Sign Language) - A form of communication generally used by deaf people or by a person who is unable to talk.

Asperger Syndrome - Until recently Asperger Syndrome was considered its own disorder. Since May 2013, with the release of the newest edition of the Diagnostic Statistic Manual, published by the American Psychiatric Association (DSM-V), it is now included as part of ASD (Autism Spectrum Disorder).

Assessments - Ways to find out what students know, and to show teachers and schools the areas in which the student needs to improve. Paper tests are most common, but there other equally good measures.

AT (Assistive Technology) - Equipment, products, and services to improve, maintain, or increase the functional capabilities of a student with a disability. This can include services to help the child, parent, or professionals who work with the child to select or use the device. It can also include training on the technology. Some examples of assistive technology are SMART Boards, iPads, laptops, DynaVox, and other voice activated computers.

Attention - The ability to focus (attend) with eyes and/or ears for a period of time without losing the meaning of what is being said.

Audiology - This can be a related service on a child's IEP. It includes the identification and determination of hearing loss and referral for the rehabilitation of hearing.

Auditory - This refers to input relating to sounds, and a child's ability to correctly perceive, discriminate, process, and respond to sounds. When this is absent, it can be an indication of a larger Sensory Processing Disorder.

Auditory Discrimination - The ability to discern likenesses or differences in sound.

Auditory Processing Disorder - See CAPD (Central Auditory Processing Disorder)

Aural - Relating to the ear or the sense of hearing.

Autism - See ASD (Autism Spectrum Disorder)

BAC (Brooklyn Autism Center) - A private independent special education school for children ages five through sixteen that utilizes Applied Behavior Analysis (ABA). (See Chapter Three *www.brooklynautismcenter.org*

BCBA (Board Certified Behavior Analyst) - A behavior analyst or therapist who meets the requirements set forth by the BACB (Behavior Analyst Certification Board). A BCBA uses direct observation and experimentation to find causes for desired and undesired behaviors. Behavior analysts design strategies to alter socially significant behavior by changing existing behaviors, teaching new behaviors, teaching what behaviors are appropriate to use in different situations, and consistently evaluating the effectiveness of their behavioral interventions. Some, but not all, ABA therapists hold BCBA certification.

Behavioral Objective - A statement of what a child will be able to do in measurable terms.

BIP (Behavior Intervention Plan) - A Behavior Intervention Plan (BIP) uses the observations made by a professional who conducted a Functional Behavior Assessment (FBA) of a child. The BIP is a specific, well-defined, written plan of action for managing a student's behavior. A BIP may include ways to change the environment to keep behavior from starting in the first place, provide positive reinforcement to promote good behavior, use planned ignoring to avoid reinforcing bad behavior, and provide supports needed so that the student will not be driven to act out due to frustration or fatigue. When a behavior plan is agreed to, it is incorporated in the child's IEP, and the school and staff are legally obligated to follow it.

BMod (Behavior Modification) - The use of empirically demonstrated behavior techniques to improve, change, or modify behavior and reactions to stimuli through positive and negative reinforcement. This is the basis for ABA therapy.

BOCES (Board of Cooperative Educational Services) - In 1948, the NYS Legislature created the Boards of Cooperative Educational Services to provide various school districts within New York State with an opportunity to share educational services. BOCES services are created when two or more school districts decide they have similar needs that can be met through a shared program. BOCES helps school districts save money by providing opportunities to pool resources and share costs. There are many BOCES programs that deal with special education students. BOCES membership is not available to the so-called "big five" city school districts: New York City, Buffalo, Rochester, Yonkers and Syracuse. Although not available in NYC, it is a very important resource if you are thinking about moving outside of NYC.

*BOE (Board of Education) - During NYC Mayor Michael Bloomberg's tenure, he dismantled the Board of Education and created the Department of Education (DOE), which is under the Mayor's direct supervision and jurisdiction.

BRP (Bay Ridge Preparatory School) - An independent private school in Brooklyn that serves special and general education students.

Burlington (Burlington School Committee v. Massachusetts Department of Education, 471 U.S. 359 (1985))** - This very important 1985 U.S.

Supreme Court decision establishes a parent's right to sue for tuition reimbursement at an approved special education school. It lays the foundation for the 1993 Supreme Court case known as "Carter" that expanded the right to sue for tuition reimbursement at independent schools as well as approved schools.

Burlington/Carter Test - See **Three-Prong Burlington/Carter Test**

Business Days - When referred to by DOE officials, or in their regulations, it means Monday through Friday, except for federal and state holidays.

CA (Chronological Age) - A child's actual age, measured by years and months. This is often used in psychological and other standardized evaluations that measure a child's academic, developmental, and language abilities against standardized norms.

CAPD (Central Auditory Processing Disorder) - This is also known as Auditory Processing Disorder or (APD). This is an umbrella term for a variety of disorders that affect the way the brain processes auditory information. It is not a sensory or inner ear hearing impairment. Children with CAPD usually have normal peripheral hearing ability. This is a complex problem affecting about five percent of school-aged children. These children cannot process the information they hear in the same way as others because their ears and brain do not fully coordinate. Children with CAPD often do not recognize subtle differences between sounds in words, even when the sounds are loud and clear enough to be heard.

Carter (Florence County School District IV v. Shannon Carter, 510 U.S. 7 (1993), 114 S. Ct. 361) - This U.S. Supreme Court decision expands the 1985 decision known as "Burlington" to include reimbursement at independent schools.

Carter Funding - This term is somewhat of a misnomer. A parent cannot simply request Carter Funding from a school district; rather, this funding comes only from a judge's order or a legal settlement agreement following the commencement of a lawsuit known as an Impartial Hearing. When this term is used it generally means the process of seeking reimbursement from a school district for a parent's unilateral placement of their disabled child in a private school when the school district fails to offer an appropriate program to that child.

*Case Manager - In New York City, this is the person at the Central Based Support Team (CBST) assigned to a child's case when the Committee on Special Education (CSE) refers a student for an approved private school. This person is responsible for matching the child with the private school.

CAT (Children's Apperception Test) - This is a projective personality test used to assess individual variations in children's responses to standardized stimuli presented in the form of pictures of animals or humans in common social situations. The purpose of this test is to assess personality, level of maturity, and, often, psychological health.

*CBST (Central Based Support Team) - The private school placement and funding offices for the NYC Department of Education. If an IEP team determines that there are no programs within the public school system that can meet the needs of a student, the team will recommend that the child's case be "Deferred to CBST for Non-Public Private School (NPS) Placement." The CBST will then review the materials and attempt to secure an appropriate NPS placement.

CBT (Cognitive Behavioral Therapy) - A psychotherapeutic approach that aims to solve problems concerning dysfunctional emotions, behaviors and cognitions through a goal-oriented systematic procedure.

CDC (Child Development Center) - An evaluation site as well as an approved preschool that is part of the Jewish Board of Family and Children's Services.

CEC (Council for Exceptional Children) - An international professional organization dedicated to improving the educational success of individuals with disabilities and/or gifted and talented students. CEC advocates for appropriate governmental policies, sets professional standards, provides professional development, advocates for individuals with exceptionalities, and helps professionals obtain the conditions and resources necessary for effective professional practice. *www.cec.sped.org*

CELF (Clinical Evaluation of Language Functioning) - A test administered by speech therapists and/or neuropsychologists as part of an evaluation to determine whether a child is in need of speech and language therapy.

Center-Based Program - An IEP recommendation for a therapeutic preschool where a toddler who has been classified by the Committee on Preschool Education (CPSE) as a "preschooler with a disability" can attend free of charge. When a child is referred to a center-based preschool, the school district pays for the school, the related services, and busing.

CFR (Code of Federal Regulations) - The administrative rules of federal agencies, which implement US statutes. The law that governs special education is known as the IDEA (Individuals with Disabilities Education Act), and the implementing regulations are found at 34 CFR Parts 300 and 301).

CHADD (Children with Attention Deficit Disorder) - A national organization providing education, advocacy, and support for individuals with ADHD. *www.chadd.org*

Chairperson - This title refers to the Chairperson of the Committee on Special Education.

*Chancellor - At the time of the publication of this book, Carmen Farina is Chancellor of the NYC DOE, overseeing over 1,800 schools with 1.1 million students, 135,000 employees, and an *operating* budget of over $23 billion. You can write to her at: CGFarina@schools.nyc.gov

*Chancellor's Regulations - Because New York City is the largest school district in the country, it has its own set of rules and regulations that govern all aspects of public schooling within the five boroughs. These regulations are divided into four sections, which are referred to as Volumes. *Volume A* addresses student-related issues, from admissions to promotion; *Volume B* addresses school-based budgeting; *Volume C* addresses employee issues, from hiring to termination; *Volume D* addresses parent and community involvement. The regulations are available in English, Arabic, Bengali, Chinese, Haitian Creole, Korean, Russian, Spanish, and Urdu. To read these Volumes in their entirety you can go to: *http://schools.nyc.gov/RulesPolicies/ChancellorsRegulations/*

Charter School - A charter school is a hybrid private/public school. They first emerged in the 1990s as a prominent and controversial idea for school reform. Charter schools are funded with public money (except for their facilities) and they are an alternative to regular public schools. A private group of people can submit and seek approval for a charter to run their own school. Charter schools are public schools that have been freed of many restrictive rules and regulations. In return, these schools are expected to achieve specific educational outcomes within a certain period (usually three to five years) or they are at risk of having their charters revoked. There is no general profile describing a typical charter school. However, it is usually smaller than a public school; sixty percent of charter schools have fewer than 200 students. They also tend to have different grade configurations than public schools and can be ungraded. Unlike public schools, some charter schools focus on a particular subject area such as math, science, the arts, or technology.

In New York City there is a school that is commonly referred to as "The Charter School" (New York Center for Autism Charter School). It is the only charter school in NYC exclusively for autistic children. Admission is solely by lottery. The school relies heavily on an ABA methodology.

Child Advocacy - An individual or organization that is engaged in advocacy, typically seeking to protect the rights of children and promote their optimal development, which, for any number of reasons, may be abridged or abused. A special education child advocate is a professional who advocates for appropriate education for children with special needs.

Classification - This is the first step in determining whether a child is eligible to receive special education services. For a preschool child there is only one classification, "Preschooler with a Disability." However, for a school-age child in New York State, there are 13 classifications. They are: Autism, Deafness, Deaf-Blindness, Emotional Disturbance (ED), Hearing Impairment, Intellectual Disability (ID), Learning Disability (LD), Multiple Disabilities, Orthopedic Impairment, Other Health Impairment (OHI), Speech or Language Impairment, Traumatic Brain Injury (TBI), and Visual Impairment.

(Note: There is no separate classification for ADHD/ADD. If this is a child's sole diagnosis, they can be classified either as: Emotional Disturbance; Learning Disabled, or Other Health Impairment. Usually a district will choose Other Health Impairment.)

Classified - An often-used term that refers to a student who has met the criteria for eligibility as a student with a disability under the IDEA and has an IEP.

CO (Counseling) - The related service of school counseling. It is usually provided in-school by either a school social worker, school psychologist, or the guidance counselor. The sessions for school-age children are usually 30 minutes in duration, or between 45-60 minutes for preschoolers. The reasoning behind the lesser amount of time for a school-age child is to avoid removing the child from the classroom for large periods of time. Counseling can be provided either individually or in a small group. When it is in a group, it is usually for no more than three children.

Cochlear Implant - A surgically implanted electronic device that provides a sense of sound to a person who is profoundly deaf or severely hard of hearing. Sometimes a cochlear implant is referred to as a bionic ear.

Cognitive Functioning - This refers to a child's level of intelligence or their IQ (Intelligence Quotient).

Commissioner of Education - Dr. John B. King, Jr. is the current Commissioner of Education for New York State. He is responsible for overseeing more than 7,000 public and independent elementary and secondary schools, which serve over 3.1 million students, as well as hundreds of other educational institutions across New York State. You can write to him at 89 Washington Avenue, Albany, New York 11234.

Commissioner's Regulations - The Regulations issued by the New York State Commissioner of Education. The section of the Commissioner's Regulations that concern special education is called Part 200.

Compensatory Education - Educational services above and beyond what is normally due to a student under state educational law. While compensatory education is not a remedy expressly indentified in the IDEA, courts have awarded it in appropriate circumstances through an Impartial Hearing or appeal. Compensatory Education may be an appropriate remedy when a student has been denied a free appropriate public education (FAPE) in past years, and can extend eligibility for special education services beyond the school year in which the student turns 21.

Congenital Disorder - Defects in or damage to a developing fetus. This may be as the result of genetic abnormalities, or something that occurred in the uterine environment, or a chromosomal abnormality. Congenital disorders vary widely in causation and in their accompanying abnormalities.

Connors Funding - This is not an official term. It has come to mean the legal process at an Impartial Hearing of requesting "direct" or "prospective" payment of tuition from a school district to a private school, available to parents who do not have the financial means to pay tuition out of pocket and seek reimbursement. The term comes from the 1988 case of Connors v. Mills, 34 F. Supp. 2d 795, from the Northern District of NY, which first discussed the possibility of this type of funding. This case has since been affirmed in the 2011 Southern District of NY case Mr. and Mrs. A v. NYC Dept. of Educ., 769 F.Supp.2d 403, which explicitly allows this type of court-ordered remedy, however, you will hear most veterans in the field still refer to these cases as "Connors."

Consent - A requirement that the school district secure the agreement of a child's parents before evaluating the child or changing that child's special education program. Consent is voluntary and may be revoked by the parent at any time.

Continuum of Services - The range of program settings into which a special education student can be placed. "The Continuum" can refer to the specific list of programs offered by a school district or to the types of settings provided in state or federal law. The list ranges from services and instructional supports designed to help a child remain in general education classes through more restrictive options that would place the child, part- or full-time, into a small special education classroom, a public special education school, or a private school, home, or hospital setting.

Cooperative Learning - An instructional approach where students learn in small, self-instructing groups, sharing responsibility for each other's learning.

COPAA (Council of Parent Attorneys and Advocates) - A nationwide group that serves not only as a training forum for attorneys and advocates, but also as an advocacy and political lobby group assuring the rights of special needs children and having these needs known on Capitol Hill. I strongly urge all my readers to support this important organization. *www.copaa.org*

Coprolalia - The excessive and uncontrollable use of foul or obscene language. Coprolalia is a typical symptom of Tourette Syndrome.

Correlation - The relationship between two scores or measures.

CP (Cerebral Palsy) - A disorder of movement, muscle tone, or posture that is caused by injury or abnormal development in the immature brain, most often before birth.

CPEL (Central Park Early Learning) - An approved preschool in Manhattan, operating under the auspices of AHRC. The CPSE makes frequent placements to this school.

CPIR (Center for Parent Information Services) - A nationwide central source of information on disabilities in infants, toddlers, children, and youth.

CPSE (Committee on Preschool Education) - This division of the CSE serves children from ages three to five. In New York City, preschool services terminate in August of the calendar year that the child actually turns five. This aging-out requirement is different in outlying suburbs.

Critical Thinking - The ability to recall information and use it to reach a logical conclusion or solve a problem.

CSE (Committee on Special Education) - Under New York law, the CSE is the group that evaluates and creates IEPs and programs for special education students. The school-age division of the CSE serves children from September of the year in which they turn 5 through the time that they either receive a bona fide high school diploma or until the end of the school year in which they turn 21, whichever comes first.

*CTT (Collaborative Team Teaching) - A term formerly used by NYC to refer to Integrated Co-Teaching (ICT) class settings. This type of class serves general and special education students. Up to 40% of the students will have IEPs and these classes have two teachers.

Cumulative File - A child's general school file maintained by the school district. Parents have the right to inspect the file and have copies of any information in it.

DAN (Defeat Autism Now) - A network of physicians, researchers, and scientists who endorse alternative, non-standard treatment for autism spectrum disorders. The organization started in 1995 under the auspices of the Autism Research Institute (ARI).

DAN Protocol - Through the use of dietary intervention, vitamin supplementation, digestive enzymes, probiotics, and even intravenous chelation, this medical treatment attempts to address biochemical irregularities in an individual. The DAN Protocol is controversial in medical circles due to a lack of empirical evidence supporting its overall efficacy. The American Academy of Pediatrics (APP) has come out against the use of chelation of autistic children.

Day Treatment - An integrated, clinical, therapeutic, and educational program jointly sponsored between a school district and a psychiatric center. This type of program serves children who require a highly structured learning environment as a result of their serious emotional disturbances. Sometimes this is also referred to as a Day Hospital.

DBT (Dialectical Behavioral Therapy) - A therapeutic methodology used to treat persons, including adolescents, with borderline personality disorder, and other emotional dysregulation and mood disorders.

Deaf-Blindness - Simultaneous hearing and visual impairments, the combination of which causes severe communication and other developmental and educational problems.

Deafness - A hearing impairment that is so severe that a child is impaired in processing linguistic information through hearing, with or without amplification, which adversely affects educational performance.

Decoding - The process of breaking down a word into understandable parts using techniques such as phonics. Word decoding is a fundamental reading skill that is tested in educational evaluations to determine a child's basic reading ability.

Development - The stages of growth from infancy through adolescence into adulthood.

Developmental Delay - Also referred to as developmental lag, where there is a delay in the appearance or acquisition of some steps or phases of growth in cognitive, fine motor, gross motor, language, self-help, or social/emotional development.

Developmental Pediatrician - A board-accredited pediatrician who additionally has sub-specialty training and certification in developmental behavioral pediatrics. This highly trained specialist focuses on assessment and treatment of children with developmental delays, developmental disabilities, and chronic conditions affecting physical or emotional development, learning, or behavior.

Diagnostic Test - A test or series of tests that can diagnose or locate areas of weakness, delays, or strengths.

DIR/Floortime - See **Floortime**

Disability - A physical, sensory, cognitive, or affective impairment that may qualify a child for the protections of federal and state laws and entitle the child to services and accommodations, including special education.

District - Shorthand for school district. In federal law, this is known as the Local Education Authority (LEA). In most of New York State, a district will encompass one or more cities or towns and is responsible for providing special education services to those students through its CSE. In New York City, the DOE is legally considered to be one school district; however, the city has chosen to divide itself into 31 geographic sub-districts, which are grouped into 10 CSE offices or "Regions." Chapter Two provides a list of all the NYC districts and regions.

*District 75 - The NYC district responsible for operating special education schools for severely disabled students who require more services than can be provided in a community school. Unlike the 31 geographic districts in NYC, District 75 is considered a city-wide "service district."

DS (Down Syndrome) - This genetic condition is also referred to as Trisomy 21. It is caused by the presence of all or part of a third copy of chromosome 21. This is the most common chromosomal abnormality in humans. It is typically associated with a delay in cognitive ability, physical growth, and a particular set of facial characteristics and health issues.

DSM-V (Diagnostic and Statistical Manual of Mental Disorders, 5th Edition) - Published by the American Psychiatric Association (APA), this book catalogues and describes all currently recognized mental health disorders. The DSM-V was published in May 2013, replacing the DSM-IV.

Due Process - In its broadest sense, this term refers to protections afforded to all citizens in many different areas of law. When referring to special education law, it usually means a Due Process Impartial Hearing. This form of dispute resolution is designed to be a fair, timely, and impartial procedure for resolving disputes arising between parents and school districts concerning the education of a student with a disability.

Dyscalculia - A specific learning disability or difficulty involving an innate inability to learn or comprehend mathematics, also referred to as a "Mathematics Disorder." The term is often used to refer specifically to the inability to perform arithmetic operations, but it is also defined as a more fundamental inability to conceptualize numbers as abstract concepts of comparative quantities.

Dysgraphia - A deficiency in the ability to write, regardless of the ability to read, which is not caused by an intellectual impairment. Children with this disorder may have other learning disabilities or ADHD. Dysgraphia is often referred to as a "Disorder of Written Expression," where a student's writing skills are substantially below what is expected.

Dyslexia - A neurologically based learning disorder that manifests itself as a difficulty with reading, spelling, and language processing, also known as a "Reading Disorder." Symptoms usually include difficulty with written and spoken information and can range from mild to debilitating. In public schools, dyslexia symptoms may be severe enough to qualify as a learning disability. However, not all school districts recognize dyslexia as a disability. Dyslexia is thought to be the result of a neurological defect or difference, but it is not an intellectual disability. Dyslexia is diagnosed in people of all levels of intelligence, including above-average intelligence.

Dysphagia - A condition in which swallowing is difficult or painful.

Early Childhood Education - The education of children from birth to eight years of age.

Echolalia - The involuntary repetition of a word or sentence just spoken by another person. This can be a symptom of autism, Asperger syndrome, Tourette syndrome, or other psychiatric disorders.

ED (Emotional Disturbance) - One of the 13 disability classifications under the IDEA. ED is defined by law as "a condition exhibiting one or more of the following characteristics over a long period of time and to a marked degree that adversely affects a child's educational performance: (a) an inability to learn that cannot be explained by intellectual, sensory, or health factors; (b) an inability to build or maintain satisfactory interpersonal relationships with peers and teachers; (c) inappropriate types of behavior or feelings under normal circumstances; (d) a general pervasive mood of unhappiness or depression; (e) a tendency to develop physical symptoms or fears associated with personal or school problems." ED includes schizophrenia but does not apply to children who are socially maladjusted, unless it is determined that they otherwise have an emotional disturbance.

EDGAR (Education Department General Administrative Regulations) - These federal regulations establish uniform administrative requirements for federal grants and agreements awarded to institutions of higher education, hospitals, and other nonprofit organizations, like schools.

EHA (Education of the Handicapped Act) - The name of the original 1975 legislation entitling students with disabilities to a free appropriate public education (FAPE). The official name of the act was changed first to the IDEA (Individuals with Disabilities Education Act), and more recently to the IDEIA (Individuals with Disabilities Education Improvement Act), although it is still commonly referred to as the IDEA.

EI (Early Intervention) - A federal program available to children from birth to age three who display a 25% delay in two or more areas of development or a 33% delay in one functional area of development.

EIP (Emergency Interim Placement) - A process in New York State permitting for the funding of an out-of-state school when there are no available in-state programs. This usually applies to residential schools. As of July 2011, NYC no longer grants this status to schools, however there is now an out-of-state approved list which can be used when no in state approved school has been secured.

Encode - The ability to express ideas in symbols or words. In the context of an educational evaluation, encoding includes the child's ability to spell.

*Enhanced Rate - When a child is issued a related service voucher (RSA) or a P-3 letter for after-school tutoring and there are no available providers who are willing to accept the standard pay rate, there is a process to get the rate increased, or "enhanced," to the customary market rate for this service.

EPC (Educational Planning Conference) - A precursor to a CSE review, where the findings of testing and evaluations are reviewed with a parent.

Equitable Considerations - This is the third prong of what is referred to as the "Carter/Burlington" test for tuition reimbursement. (See Chapter Four)

ESL (English as a Second Language) - A service available to children when English is not their first language. Children are taken out of their regular classrooms to study English. This is not a special education service.

ESY (Extended School Year) - See 12-MSY

EVS (Education Vision Services) - Sometimes referred to as "Vision Services," offered to children with visual impairments.

Executive Functioning - A set of behaviors that allow us to plan, organize, and monitor our performances in the world. This includes skills that allow us to sequence information, inhibit one response in favor of another, plan before acting, switch between ideas, generate ideas, balance speed and accuracy, solve abstract problems, and multi-task. Students with executive functioning difficulties often present as disorganized and inattentive.

Expanded Rate - When the DOE pays more than the contracted rate to a SETSS provider.

Expressive Language - The ability to communicate by using words, writing, or gestures.

Extended School Day - A provision for students, both general and special education, to receive instruction for a period longer than the usual school day.

FAPE (Free Appropriate Public Education) - This is a cornerstone of special education law and policy. It is the description of the special education that must be provided to every eligible student with a disability. The term is found in the Individuals with Disabilities Education Act (IDEA) and Section 504 of the Rehabilitation Act of 1973, guaranteeing the rights of children with disabilities in the United States. Under the IDEA, FAPE is defined as an educational program that is individualized to a specific child, designed to meet that child's unique needs, provide access to the general curriculum, meet the grade-level standards established by the state, and from which the child receives educational benefit. Under Section 504, FAPE is defined as "the provision of regular or special education and related aids and services that are designed to meet individual needs of handicapped persons as well as the needs of non-handicapped persons based on adherence to procedural safeguards outlined in the law." The United States Department of Education issues regulations that define and govern the provision of FAPE.

FAS (Fetal Alcohol Syndrome) - A pattern of physical and mental defects that can develop in a fetus in association with high levels of alcohol consumption during pregnancy.

FBA (Functional Behavioral Assessment) - An assessment of a child whose behaviors interfere with classroom functioning. Conducted by a licensed psychologist who must follow clear regulations about how the assessment should be done, it is used to create a Behavior Intervention Plan (BIP) that becomes part of the IEP.

Feeding Therapy - A form of therapy provided by speech therapists or other medical providers to infants and children who present any of a wide array of feeding difficulties such as: reduced or limited intake; food refusal; food selectivity (type and or texture); dysphagia (swallowing difficulty); oral motor deficits; delayed feeding development; food or swallowing phobias; and mealtime tantrums.

FERPA (Family Educational Rights and Privacy Act) - A federal law regulating the management of student records and disclosure of information from these records. This legislation gives parents the right to inspect and review their child's educational records, to amend errors or inaccuracies in those records, and to consent to disclosure of records.

Fine Motor - Functions that require tiny muscle movements, for example writing or drawing.

Floortime (or DIR/Floortime) - A form of play therapy developed by child psychiatrist Dr. Stanley Greenspan using interactions and relationships to teach children with developmental delays, including autism. This approach is based on the theory that autistic symptoms are caused by problems with brain processing affecting a child's relationships as well as their senses. Sometimes this method is also referred to as DIR (Developmental, Individual Difference, and Relationship-Based Therapy) or DIR/Floortime.

*FNR (Final Notice of Recommendation) - In NYC, this specific form is issued after an IEP meeting and informs parents of the specific school program being recommended and its location. Since a specific time frame is attached to the issuance of this recommendation, it is advised that parents save the envelope in which this notice arrives.

FOIA (Freedom of Information Act) - Enacted in 1966, FOIA affords any person the right to request access to federal agency records or information, with certain exceptions.

FSIQ (Full Scale Intelligence Quotient) - The weighted average of the scores from all the sub-tests of an IQ or intelligence test. This is the score commonly known as an IQ score. It can be an inaccurate assessment of a student's intelligence if there are large disparities between sub-tests.

GE (Grade Equivalent) - These numbers often appear on an IEP or an educational evaluation, indicating what grade and month in that grade a child is scoring or functioning on in a specific educational area. For example a GE of 2.9 in mathematic calculation means that in mathematic calculation, the child is scoring in the 9th month of the 2nd grade. It is the average raw score for all children in the same school based on national norms. It is only a rough estimate of a child's mastery of academic work or capacity to learn, but it is relied upon heavily by school districts.

GLC (General Language Composite) - A measure of expressive and receptive vocabulary ability.

Hearing - When this term is being used by a CSE or school district, it usually means an Impartial or Due Process Hearing (as opposed to the physical sense of hearing).

Hearing Impaired - An impairment in hearing, whether permanent or fluctuating, which adversely affects a child's educational performance, but is not included under the definition of deafness.

*HES (Hearing Education Services) - In NYC, a separate office that provides in-school services to students with hearing impairments.

Home Instruction - Part of the continuum of educational services that can be provided by a school district when a child is either too ill to attend school or is awaiting a placement and cannot remain in their prior public school placement. A licensed teacher will come to the child's home for one to two hours per day. The service can also be performed at a library or other public area. The fact that a child is a special education student does not mean that the teacher provided is a licensed special education teacher.

Home Program - Educational and related services that are provided to the child at home or in the community, either in lieu of a center-based school program or as a complement to a school program. For CPSE students, Special Education Itinerant Teacher (SEIT) services fall under this category. A SEIT can work with a child either in their home or at the mainstream school/program that the child attends. Similarly related services (ST, OT, PT, CO) can be provided to the child in their home, in a sensory gym, or in the provider's office.

Home Schooling - Parents of mainstream children, as well as special needs children, have the right to choose to educate their child at home as long as they adhere to the required detailed regulations of their school district. Parents must file a notice of intent to home-school their child, as well as submitting an educational plan and periodic reports. Parents who home-school their special needs child are entitled to receive the related services mandated on their child's IEP.

Hyperacusis - An oversensitivity to sound arising from a problem in the way the brain's central auditory processing center perceives noise. This is often seen in children who have other sensory problems.

Hypotonia - A childhood disorder commonly referred to as "low muscle tone."

ICT (Integrated Co-Teaching) - An inclusion class consisting of no more than 12 special education students in a classroom being taught alongside general education students. These classes are co-taught by a special education and a general education teacher. Generally no more than 40% of the students in an ICT class are special education. An ICT class is considered to be part of a general education curriculum.

IDEA (Individuals with Disabilities Education Act) - The federal law governing special education in the US. The IDEA grants services to children with disabilities. This is the cornerstone of all special education in the United States of America. Officially, it is now called the Individual with Disabilities Education Improvement Act (IDEIA); however, everyone still refers to it as the IDEA.

IEE (Independent Educational Evaluation) - An evaluation conducted by a qualified examiner who is *not* employed by the school district responsible for the education of the child. A parent may request an IEE for their child at public expense if they disagree with the findings of an evaluation conducted by the school district, however, the district may seek to limit the cost of this evaluation or may request an Impartial Hearing to show why it should not be required to provide an IEE.

IEP (Individual Education Program) - A written document mandated by the IDEA, when a child has been found eligible for a special education program and/or services. The IEP reflects the student's areas of need, based on parent and teacher reports and the results of formal evaluations. It then sets goals and objectives that the student will be expected to achieve within one year for each area of need. Finally, the IEP will recommend the programs, services, and accommodations that the student requires to meet those goals. An IEP should describe how the student learns, how the student best demonstrates that learning, and what teachers and service providers will do to help the student learn more effectively. As long as a student qualifies for special education, the IEP must be annually updated. The public program to which the student is assigned is required to follow and comply with every provision in the IEP.

IEP Team - The group of people mandated to participate at an IEP meeting in order to develop the IEP and make a program recommendation. In New York, this is sometimes referred to as the CSE Team or Review Team. Federal and state law list an assortment of professionals that are generally required to attend an IEP meeting, including a school psychologist, the student's general and/or special education teacher or service provider, and a school district representative. The student's parents must always be invited to the meeting, though the team must still meet if the parents refuse or decline to attend. The parents may also bring to the meeting any other person who has knowledge of, or special expertise regarding, the student, including professionals who have worked with the student, friends or family members, and an advocate or attorney. Parents may bring the student to the meeting if they choose, and, in the case of a student aged 15 or older, the district must invite the student to attend.

IESP (Individualized Education Service Program) - A plan created for a student who is eligible for special education services, resides in New York State, and is placed in a non-public school (usually a mainstream or parochial school.) Not to be used if a parent is seeking tuition reimbursement for a private special education school.

IFSP (Individualized Family Service Plan) - A written document that outlines the services a child and their family will receive through the federal program known as Early Intervention.

IHO (Impartial Hearing Officer) - The person who sits as a judge at a due process impartial hearing, taking evidence, hearing testimony, and rendering a written decision either in favor of the parent or the school district. In New York City, an IHO is an attorney, however, outside of NYC, they can be former school officials (e.g., a retired superintendent), or other laypersons who pass an examination.

Impartial Hearing - A legal proceeding used to resolve disputes between parents and a school district regarding issues related to special education. Sometimes this is referred to as a Due Process Hearing or a Due Process Impartial Hearing or just a Hearing. Impartial Hearings involve many strict procedures, and while parents may represent themselves and their child at such hearings, they may also be represented by an attorney or advocate. The proceeding is commenced by the filing of a Request for an Impartial Hearing (IHR), alternatively referred to as a Due Process Complaint (DPC). The school district may be represented at a hearing by an attorney or by a non-attorney representative.

Impartial Hearing Decision - A written decision rendered by the impartial hearing officer at the conclusion of a hearing, finding either in favor of the parent or the school district.

Inclusion - The educational practice of educating children with disabilities in classrooms with children without disabilities, also known as "mainstreaming."

Independent School - A private school that does not have a contract with the New York State Education Department to provide special education services through a school district's placement process. These are sometimes also known as "non-approved schools," however, this term has no relation to the private school's accreditation.

Interactive Metronome - A computer based therapy used to enhance motor planning, sequencing, and timing. This therapy is usually administered by an occupational therapist certified in this methodology.

Interim IEP - An IEP developed pending a permanent placement. This is often used when a child is awaiting a private school placement or has to be placed on home instruction. An interim IEP is supposed to be reviewed every three months.

Intelligence - The ability to learn from experience and apply it in the future to solve problems and make judgments.

IQ (Intelligence Quotient) - A way of expressing the results of an intelligence test through a quantified score.

*Jose P. - A class action lawsuit involving the rights of disabled students to be referred, evaluated, and placed in a timely fashion into appropriate educational programs and services in New York City public schools. As a result of this lawsuit, a judgment was issued in 1979 by the presiding judge, Eugene Nickerson, directing a variety of relief measures. There have been several subsequent orders and stipulations issued since 1979.

Advocates for Children, the premier public advocacy agency in NYC, continues to monitor the implementation of the Jose P. judgment and orders.

Kinesthetic - An ability to learn through body movements.

KTEA (Kaufman Test of Educational Achievement) - An educational test that covers areas mandated by the IDEA and is often used by school districts to measure a child's academic levels of functioning.

LD (Learning Disability) - A general term that describes a variety of learning problems. It is also one of the 13 disability classifications defined by the IDEA as *a disorder in one or more of the basic psychological processes involved in understanding or in using language, spoken or written, that may manifest itself in an imperfect ability to listen, think, speak, read, write, spell, or do mathematical calculations, including conditions such as perceptual disabilities, brain injury, minimal brain dysfunction.*

LDA (Learning Disability Association of America) - Founded in 1963, LDA provides support to people with learning disabilities, their parents, teachers, and other professionals.

LEA (Local Educational Agency) - The term used by federal law to refer to the local school district.

Learning Styles - This refers to the fact that individuals process and perceive information in different ways.

Lindamood Bell - Founded in 1986 by Patricia Lindamood and Nanci Bell, Lindamood Bell is a nationally acclaimed program designed to individually teach children and adults to read, spell, comprehend, think critically, and express through language.

LRE (Least Restrictive Environment) - The IDEA (and all special education law) requires that every student with a disability be educated in the "least restrictive environment" in which he or she can make meaningful educational progress. To the greatest extent possible, students with disabilities should be placed in general education classrooms alongside students without disabilities. *www.lrecoalition.org*

Mainstreaming - Where a child with an IEP has an opportunity to be educated with or alongside typically developing, non-special education students in a regular classroom for a portion of each school day. It also refers to opportunities for participating with typical children in non-academic activities, such as lunch, art, music, assembly, and trips.

Manifestation Determination Review - A meeting of the IEP team, which occurs when a child with a disability acts out in school, or violates a school rule, resulting in suspension for 10 or more days in a school year (cumulative days, not necessarily consecutive days). The meeting is a review of whether or not the child's behavior was caused by or is directly related to his/her disability (i.e. manifestation of the disability). Behaviors are a manifestation of a child's disability if those behaviors are caused by, or are directly related to, the student's disabilities or if such conduct was a direct result of the school district's failure to implement the student's Individualized Education Plan (IEP).

MCC (Manhattan Children's Center) - A private independent school for autistic children. (See Chapter Three)

MD (Muscular Dystrophy) - A group of muscle diseases in which the face, arm, leg, spine, or heart muscles gradually shrink and weaken over time.

Mediation - A voluntary dispute resolution process. Federal and state law provide for mediation with a neutral third-party facilitator to address special education disputes between parents and school districts, either as an alternative to an Impartial Hearing or as part of that process. Unlike an Impartial Hearing, however, mediation can only produce an agreement between parties; there is no order by a judge.

Medicaid Waiver - A New York State program permitting children with significant developmental disabilities or intellectual challenges resulting in a low IQ to receive Medicaid and other funded services. This program is not based on parental income and resources.

MMFS (Mary McDowell Friends School) - A private independent special education school in Brooklyn. (See Chapter Three)

Modifications - This term may be used to describe a change in curriculum for students who may be unable to comprehend all of the content an instructor is teaching. This includes changes in instructional level, content, and performance criteria. It may also include changes in a test form or format, or alternative assignments.

MR (Mental Retardation) - This term is no longer used by school districts or public agencies, and has been replaced by ID (Intellectually Disabled). This is a developmental disability that first appears in children under the age of 18. It is defined as an intellectual functioning level (as measured by standard tests for intelligence quotient) that is well below average and significantly limits daily living skills (adaptive functioning).

Multisensory - Relating to or involving several bodily senses, and most often used to describe a type of learning that involves receiving information using more than one sense.

Multisensory teaching - An approach to teaching that combines and engages three learning senses: auditory (hearing and speaking), visual (seeing and perceiving), and kinesthetic (touch and movement). Lessons are taught using two or more of these modalities simultaneously to receive or express information. Teachers teach in two or more ways and students can express their responses in a variety of ways.

NAMI (National Alliance for the Mentally Ill) - The nation's largest grassroots mental health organization dedicated to building better lives for the millions of Americans affected by mental illness. NAMI advocates for access to services, treatment, support, and research.

NCLB (No Child Left Behind) - A 2001 Congressional Act, which took effect in 2002, enacting theories of standard- based educational reforms. Its purpose was to hold states, school districts, and individual schools responsible for improving academic performance. The law requires states to establish rigorous academic standards, conduct annual assessments, and implement a comprehensive accountability system.

NCSET (National Center on Secondary Education and Transition) - A federally funded center that coordinates national resources, offers technical assistance, and disseminates information related to secondary education and transition for students with disabilities, in order to create opportunities for youth to achieve successful futures.

NEPSY - A neuropsychological test used in various combinations to assess development in children ages 3–16 years. The test examines six functional domains: attention and executive functions; language and communication; sensorimotor functions; visuospatial functions; learning; and memory.

*NEST - A highly coveted NYC public school inclusion program for children with high functioning autism or Asperger syndrome. The program begins for kindergarten-age children. The classes generally have 12 children in the lower grades, half with IEPs and half typically developing children without IEPs.

Neurologist - A medical doctor who is trained in the diagnosis and treatment of nervous system disorders, including diseases of the brain, spinal cord, nerves, and muscles.

*Nickerson Letter - An often-used euphemism for a voucher enabling an eligible student to attend an approved private special education school for one year, when the district fails to adhere to a strict timeline for placement. Its official name is a P-1 letter. (See Chapter Three)

NLD or NVLD (Nonverbal Learning Disorder or Nonverbal Learning Disability) - A neurological disorder that is characterized by a significant discrepancy between high verbal and lower performance scores on an IQ test. This condition is highlighted by deficits in motor, visuospatial, executive functioning, and social skills. NLD involves deficits in perception, coordination, socialization, and non-verbal problem solving.

NORD (National Organization for Rare Disorders) - A federation of voluntary health organizations dedicated to helping people with rare "orphan" diseases and assisting the organizations that serve them. A rare disorder is considered to be a disease affecting fewer than 200,000 Americans. There are nearly 7000 such diseases affecting nearly 30 million Americans.

Norm - A statistical term used to describe the performance of some specified group. The term "norm" indicates "normal," usual, or average performance.

NRT (Norm Referenced Tests) - These types of tests compare each student's score to the scores of students who took the same exams before. Questions are usually based on the content of nationally used textbooks, not what is being taught locally.

NYCA (New York Collaborates for Autism) - A New York City organization involved in creating model programs that educate and serve children on the autistic spectrum and their families. Their mission is to develop programs that provide individuals and families living with Autism Spectrum Disorder (ASD) with access to comprehensive evidence-based educational services, support the development of community resources, support individuals with ASD, and coordinate and facilitate ongoing research into ASD. It is the parent organization for the NYCA Charter School. *www.nyc4a.org*

*NYCA Charter School (New York Center for Autism Charter School) - This model charter school opened in September 2005 and is dedicated exclusively to providing education to students with ASD. Admission is free of charge, limited, and on a lottery basis.

NYCLI (New York Child Learning Institute) - An approved private school for autistic children. (See Chapter Three)

Objective Test - A psychological test that measures an individual's characteristics in a way that is independent of rater bias or an examiner's own beliefs.

OCD (Obsessive Compulsive Disorder) - A mental disorder that is characterized by intrusive thoughts (obsessions) that produce anxiety, by repetitive behaviors (compulsions), which are aimed at reducing anxiety, or by combinations of such thoughts and behaviors.

OCR (U.S. Office of Civil Rights) - This federal sub-agency is part of the U.S. Department of Education. It is charged with the oversight of several civil rights laws that prohibit discrimination in programs or activities that receive federal financial assistance from the U.S. Department of Education, including Section 504 of the Rehabilitation Act of 1973, which prohibits discrimination on the basis of disability.

ODD (Oppositional Defiant Disorder) - A condition in which a child displays an ongoing pattern of uncooperative, defiant, hostile, and annoying behavior toward people in authority. The child's behavior often disrupts the child's normal daily activities, including activities within the family and at school.

OG (Orton Gillingham) - A flexible instructional approach to teaching reading, spelling, and writing that uses an intensive, sequential phonics-based system teaching the basics of word formation before meanings. The method utilizes the three learning modalities, or pathways, through which people learn—visual, auditory, and kinesthetic. This approach is most often utilized for students with dyslexia. *www.orton-gillingham.us*

OHI (Other Health Impairment) - One of the 13 CSE Classifications, OHI refers to a child having limited strength, vitality or alertness, including a heightened alertness to environmental stimuli, resulting in limited alertness with respect to the educational environment, that (1) is due to chronic or acute health problems such as asthma, attention deficit disorder or attention deficit hyperactivity disorder, diabetes, epilepsy, a heart condition, hemophilia, lead poisoning, leukemia, nephritis, rheumatic fever, and sickle cell anemia; and (2) adversely affects a child's educational performance.

Olfactory - Pertaining to a child's ability to correctly perceive, discriminate, process, and respond to different odors. When a child cannot do this, it can be a symptom of a sensory processing disorder.

On-Task Behavior - Expected behavior at that moment on that particular task.

*OPTS (Office of Pupil Transportation Services) - As the name implies, this is the central office which coordinates busing services and school transportation for students attending both public and non-public schools located within the five boroughs and neighboring counties in New York, New Jersey, and Connecticut. Sometimes it is referred to as OPS. *http:// schools.nyc.gov/Offices/Transportation/default.htm* (718 392 8855)

OPWDD (Office of People with Developmental Disabilities) - The New York State agency responsible for coordinating services for more than 126,000 New Yorkers with developmental disabilities, including intellectual disabilities, cerebral palsy, Down syndrome, autism spectrum disorder, and other disabilities. This agency provides services directly and through a network of approximately 700 nonprofit service providing agencies, with about 80 percent of services provided by the private nonprofits, and 20 percent provided by state-run services. *www.opwdd.ny.gov*

Oral - A child's ability to correctly perceive, discriminate, process, and respond to input in the mouth. Difficulty with this can be an indication of a sensory processing disorder.

Oromotor Dysfunction - The inability to control the muscles of the mouth, including the tongue and lips, and the inability to control swallowing. This condition can impede speech and cause excessive drooling.

Orthopedic Impairment - As defined in the Regulations of the New York State Commissioner of Education, this term means a severe orthopedic impairment that adversely affects a child's educational performance. The term includes impairments caused by a congenital anomaly (e.g. clubfoot, absence of some member, etc.), impairments caused by disease (e.g., poliomyelitis, bone tuberculosis), and impairments from other causes (e.g., cerebral palsy, amputations, and fractures or burns which cause contractures).

OSEP (United States Office of Special Education Programs) - This Office is dedicated to improving opportunities for infants, toddlers, children, and youth with disabilities, ages birth through age 21, by providing leadership and financial support to assist states and local districts. OSEP administers the Individuals with Disabilities Education Act (IDEA).

OSERS (United States Office of Special Education and Rehabilitative Services) - A federal agency which is part of the government's executive branch within the Department of Education.

*OSIS Number - Every student in the NYC school system has a nine-digit number also referred to as a student identification number. This number appears on the first page of an IEP and is also located on a student's permanent school records.

OSR (Office of State Review) - This New York State agency based in Albany was created in 1990 to assist New York State Review Officers (SROs). It is this agency that publishes the appeal decisions from Impartial Hearings. *www.sro.nysed.gov*

OT (Occupational Therapy) - The use of treatments to develop, re-cover, or maintain the daily living skills of children with a physical, mental, or developmental condition. Occupational therapy interventions help children with various needs to improve their cognitive, physical, and motor skills and enhance their self-esteem and sense of accomplishment. The treatment helps in adapting to the environment, modifying the task, teaching the skill, and educating the child and parents in order to increase participation in and performance of a variety of daily activities, including school performance.

*P-1 Letter - The official name for a Nickerson Letter. It is a voucher which entitles the student to placement in a NYS-approved non-public school at public expense when the district fails to adhere to a strict timeline of evaluation and placement. (See Chapter Three)

*P-2 Letter - When an approved non-public school accepts a student pursuant to a P-1 letter, the school must return a letter of acceptance, known as a P-2 letter, to the CSE. The P-2 letter confirms to the CSE the date on which enrollment begins, the size of the classroom the student is placed in, the age range of the students in the class, as well as the related services provided to the student. Like the P-1 letter, it is only used in New York City.

*P-3 Letter - If a child has been recommended to receive Special Education Teacher Support Services (SETSS) but the NYC DOE is unable to provide the service, a P-3 letter enables the parent to obtain this service for their child from an eligible independent provider at DOE expense. There are strict conditions as to when this is granted and generally it is not awarded to a student who attends a public school. It is most often given to children whose parents place them in mainstream private schools and do not sue for tuition reimbursement. When a P-3 letter is granted, it is accompanied by a list of approved providers.

PAF (Preventing Academic Failure) - A program for teaching reading, spelling, and handwriting in grades K-3. It prevents or addresses reading failure in learning disabled and struggling readers.

Palilalia - A pathological condition in which a word or phrase is rapidly and involuntarily repeated or the echoing of one's own spoken words. It may sound like stuttering. It is a complex tic similar to echolalia and coprolalia and can be a symptom of Tourette syndrome or Asperger syndrome or autism.

Parent Member - A member of a CSE review team who resides within NYC and has a child in special education. This person is different from the child's own parent. The Parent Member is not a mandated or required member of a review team, but must be present if the parent requests this in writing 72 hours before the actual meeting.

Parent Training and Information Centers - Programs funded by the Office of Special Education Programs in the U.S. Department of Education for the purpose of providing training and information to meet the needs of parents of children with disabilities living in the area served by the center. In New York, the two federally funded agencies that do this are: Advocates for Children of New York (*www.advocatesforchildren.org*) and Resources for Children with Special Needs (*www.includenyc.org*).

Parental Placement - When a parent chooses to enroll their child in a private mainstream school, including but not limited to a parochial school, without the intent to seek tuition reimbursement from the school district. This is not the same as a unilateral placement. In NYC, this often triggers the issuance of an Individualized Education Services Plan (IESP) as opposed to an IEP.

Parents Guide to Special Education - A New York State publication given to a parent at their initial social history interview, usually done by a CSE social worker. This booklet outlines the process of evaluation, review, placement, Impartial Hearings, appeals, and parents' rights. It is available online at: *http://www.p12.nysed.gov/specialed/publications/policy/parentguide.htm*.

Part 200 - New York State Regulations of the Commissioner of Education for Students with Disabilities.

Part 201 - New York State Regulations of the Commissioner of Education - Procedural Safeguards for Students with Disabilities Subject to Discipline.

PDD (Pervasive Developmental Disorder) - The class of conditions or developmental disorder to which autism belongs.

PDD NOS (Pervasive Developmental Disorder, Not Otherwise Specified) - See Autism Spectrum Disorder

Pendency - A parent has the right to challenge decisions made by a school district which affects their child's education. To do this a parent or their legal representative files a request for an Impartial Hearing. When a written request for Impartial Hearing is filed, the child has the right to "Stay Put" in his or her current educational placement at district expense, unless the child's parents and school district agree otherwise, until the Impartial Hearing and all appeals are concluded. The purpose of pendency is to provide stability and consistency in the education of a child with a disability. It is also referred to as the "Stay Put provision" of the IDEA. (See Chapter Four)

Percentile - A score that reflects a comparison of one child's performance with others who took the same test.

Percentile Rank - A point in a distribution of scores.

Perception - The mental ability to grasp or understand objects by means of the senses.

PIQ (Performance Intelligence Quotient) - A measure of fluid reasoning, spatial processing, attentiveness to detail, and visual motor integration. It focuses on perceptual organization, such as the ability to think in visual images and to manipulate these images with ease, to reason without the use of words, to interpret visual material, and nonverbal learning and memory.

Performance Standards - What a student is supposed to be able to do by the end of a particular grade.

Phonemic Awareness - The ability to hear, identify, and manipulate phonemes, in order to teach the correspondence between these sounds and the spelling patterns that represent words.

Phonemes - A speech sound that distinguishes one word from another.

Phonics - A method for teaching, reading, and writing of the English language, by developing phonemic awareness. The goal of phonics is to enable beginning readers to decode new written words by sounding them out, or in phonics terms, *blending* the sound-spelling patterns. Since the turn of the 20th century, phonics has been widely used in primary education and in teaching literacy throughout the English-speaking world.

Physiatrist - A medical doctor who manages children with traumatic brain injury, congenital and acquired amputations, as well as both acute and long-term spinal cord injury. These doctors also manage children with muscle diseases such as Duchenne muscular dystrophy and spinal muscular atrophy, pediatric burns, and a myriad of congenital disabilities. Using medication and physical therapy, physiatrists participate in the care of children with these neuro-muscular conditions.

Placement - The setting in which special education services are delivered to a student.

PLI (Pragmatic Language Impairment) - An impairment in understanding pragmatic areas of language. This type of impairment was previously called "semantic-pragmatic disorder (SPD)." Pragmatic language impairments are related to autism. Individuals with these impairments have special challenges with the meaning of what is being said and using language appropriately in social situations.

Pragmatic Language - This broadly refers to social language and using language appropriately in social situations. A person with pragmatic language problems may say inappropriate or unrelated things during a conversation, tell stories in a disorganized way, or have very little variety in language use.

Preschool Pendency - This applies when a child, at five years of age, leaves the auspices of the CPSE and enters the school-age CSE. If a parent disagrees with the IEP or the placement being recommended at the Turning Five Review Meeting, the parent's recourse is to file for an Impartial Hearing. Once the hearing request is filed, the child's "Stay Put" or pendency placement is in place for the duration of the hearing, and any subsequent appeal, since this was the last-agreed-to placement by both the parents and the school district. Pendency does not apply when a child is leaving Early Intervention and entering CPSE.

Preschooler with a Disability - A generic classification used by the CPSE for a preschool-age child who meets criteria for classification as a student with a disability. The criteria requires that a child exhibits or tests with a significant delay or disability in one or more functional areas related to cognitive, language and communicative, adaptive, socio-emotional, or motor development, which adversely affects the student's ability to learn. The child's delay or disability must be documented by the results of an individual evaluation done in the child's native language and at no cost to the parents. The evaluation includes, but is not limited to, information in all functional areas obtained from a structured observation of a student's performance and behavior, a parental interview, and other individually administered assessment procedures, and, when reviewed in combination and compared to accepted milestones for child development, indicate: (a) a 12-month delay in one or more functional area(s); or (b) a 33 percent delay in one functional area or a 25 percent delay in each of two functional areas; or (c) if appropriate standardized instruments are individually administered in the evaluation process, a score of 2.0 standard deviations below the mean in one functional area, or a score of 1.5 standard deviations below the mean in each of two functional areas.

Prior Written Notice - Required written notice sent to parents when a school proposes to initiate or change (or refuses to initiate or change) the identification, evaluation, or placement of a child.

PSQ (Processing Speed Quotient) - Part of an IQ test that measures fine-motor coordination, motivation, attention, concentration, distractibility, visual memory, planning ability, the ability to process abstract symbols, and how quickly one processes information.

Procedural Safeguards Notice - Notice provided to parents and school districts at the beginning and during the special education process. This notice specifically informs parents of their legal rights under federal and state law so that they may be informed about and involved in the special education process and decisions, assuring that their child receives a free appropriate public education (FAPE). These procedural safeguards include: prior written notice of all meetings and decisions made by the school district, notice of the availability and use of mediation, and due process in resolving disputes.

Proficiency - The mastery of, or the ability to do, something at grade level.

Projective Tests - These tests are largely based on Freudian psychology and seek to expose the unconscious perceptions of people. Projective tests purportedly expose certain aspects of the personality of individuals that are impossible to measure by means of an objective test, and are supposedly more reliable at uncovering "protected" or unconscious personality traits or features. These types of tests are designed to let a person respond to ambiguous stimuli, presumably revealing hidden emotions and internal conflicts. Some private special education schools require such tests as part of their admission procedures.

PROMPT Therapy (Prompts for Restructuring Oral Muscular Phonetic Targets) - A technique or therapy approach that uses tactile-kinesthetic articulatory cues (PROMPTs) on the jaw, face, and under the chin, to develop or restructure speech production. A PROMPT-trained speech-language pathologist helps to manually guide articulators to help a child produce specific sounds or words. The clinician uses his or her hands to cue and stimulate articulatory movement, and at the same time helps the child eliminate any unnecessary movements.

Proprioception - The sense of "position," meaning one's sense of the relative position of neighboring parts of the body and strength of effort being employed in movement; as well as a sense of input from the muscles and joints about body position, weight, pressure, stretch, movement and changes in position. When a child has difficulty with this, it can be a symptom of a sensory processing disorder.

Prospective Funding - When a school district agrees to pay a private special education school prospectively (going forward) rather than reimburse a parent for monies the parent has already paid. (See Connors Funding)

Psychiatrist - A medical doctor who has completed medical school, and specializes in psychiatry, and is certified in treating mental disorders. Psychiatrists are trained in diagnostic evaluation and in psychotherapy. They can prescribe and monitor medication as well as conduct physical examinations, order and interpret laboratory tests and electroencephalograms, and order brain-imaging studies.

Psychologist - A non-medical professional who studies mental processes and human behavior by observing, interpreting, and recording how people relate to one another and the environment. A school psychologist can have either a master's-level or doctoral degree. When working in a school setting, a psychologist will do testing and evaluations, provide counseling, and collaborate with educators, parents, and other professionals. Most often a school psychologist is the person on the CSE evaluation team who administers the psycho-educational test, which is a combination of intelligence and academic testing. This test is used to evaluate eligibility for special education, determine social/emotional development, and the mental health status of a child.

PT (Physical Therapy) - School-based physical therapy services address mobility throughout the educational environment. Issues with mobility may include balance, strength, and/or endurance in regard to walking (with or without an assistive device) or negotiating a wheelchair. The general goal is to make mobility as safe and independent as possible, as well as address any positioning needs as they pertain to maintaining range of motion, weight bearing, and strength for mobility.

Pull-Out Services - When a child is removed from his or her regular or special education classroom to receive mandated related services.

*RASE - Regional Administrator of Special Education

RCT (Regents Competency Test) - A less rigorous version of the high school Regents Exam.

Readiness Test - A test that ascertains whether a learner is "ready" for certain school tasks.

Receptive Language - The comprehension of language by listening and understanding what is communicated. Another way to view it is as the receiving aspect of language.

*Region - Legally, New York City is only one school district. However, because of its enormous size, it has chosen to divide itself into ten regions, which encompass various smaller districts.

Related Service - The IDEA defines related services as: *transportation and such developmental, corrective, and other supportive services as are required to assist a child with a disability to benefit from special education...* [Section 300.24(a)]. Students who require special education and specially designed instruction are eligible for related services under the IDEA. Related services include: audiology, counseling services, early identification, family training-counseling and home visits, health services, medical services, nursing services, nutrition services, occupational therapy, orientation and mobility services, parent counseling and training, physical therapy, psychological services, recreation and therapeutic recreation, rehabilitative counseling services, school health services, service coordination services, social work services in schools, speech pathology and speech-language pathology, transportation and related costs, and assistive technology and services.

Reliability - When referring to reliability in educational terms it generally means the measure of the worth of a specific test. In other words, whether the test actually and consistently measures what it was intended to measure.

Remedial Services (or Remediation) - Process by which a student identified as performing below grade level in reading, writing, or mathematics, receives extra support and instruction in an effort to develop or strengthen these skills. The student does not have to be classified or have an IEP in order to receive remedial services.

ResHab (Residential Habilitation) - A service for individuals with disabilities, including children who hold a Medicaid waiver. The service is usually provided in their home and assists the parents in caring for their disabled child.

Resolution Session - After an Impartial Hearing Request has been filed, and before the commencement of the Impartial Hearing, there is a mandatory resolution period. The school district must convene a meeting with the parents who filed for the hearing for the purpose of trying to resolve the issue. Cases in which a parent seeks tuition reimbursement cannot be resolved at a resolution session.

Resource Room Placement - A special education placement where a child is generally pulled out of class for at least one period per day and given small group instruction by a special education teacher. This can appear on a child's IEP, but can also be provided to a student who is at risk and does not have an IEP. In New York City, this is now called SETSS (Special Education Teacher Support Services), which can be provided to a child within the classroom setting.

Resources for Children with Special Needs - A nonprofit NYC-based organization whose mission is to serve families of children and young adults with all special needs. They provide individual advocacy, specialized training, and community awareness events. This organization is one of the country's 100 federally funded Parent Training and Information Centers. *www.includenyc.org*

Respite Care - A service provided to families of children who require extraordinary forms of care so that the family can handle their own business affairs, take vacations, and have some relief from the duties of caring for such a disabled child. It is often provided through the Medicaid waiver program and is potentially available for the parents of disabled children, age three and younger, under the Early Intervention Program.

*RSA (Related Service Authorization) - A voucher issued by the district when a contracted agency cannot provide a mandated service. This voucher enables a child to receive private, after-school related services but only through approved providers appearing on a list promulgated by the school district.

RTC (Residential Treatment Center) - A live-in placement for children with serious emotional disturbances. It is considered the most restrictive of placements since it requires removing the child from their home and community.

RTI (Response to Intervention) - A method of academic intervention that provides early systematic assistance to children who are having difficulty learning. RTI seeks to prevent academic failure through early intervention, frequent progress measurement, and increasingly intensive research-based instructional interventions for children who continue to have difficulty.

*SBST (School Based Support Team) - A team of professionals found in every public school who are part of the CSE and perform the same evaluative and review functions.

School Report Card - New York State Report Cards provide enrollment, demographic, attendance, suspension, dropout, teacher assessment, accountability, graduation rate, post-graduate plan, and fiscal data for public and charter schools, districts, and the State. *reportcards.nysed.gov*

SEA (State Education Agency) - A state-level government agency charged with providing information, resources, and assistance on educational matters to schools, parents, and residents. In New York State, our SEA is the State Education Department (NYSED) located at: 89 Washington Avenue, Albany, New York 12234.

§ (Section Symbol) - This is the symbol used to denote a specific section of a document, statute, or legal regulation, rule, or code.

Section 504 - This refers to a provision of the Rehabilitation Act of 1973, which prohibits discrimination against any person with disabilities by recipients of federal funds.

Sialorrhea - Excessive drooling or salivation, a common problem in neurologically impaired children, or children with hypotonia (low muscle tone).

SED (Serious Emotional Disturbance) - This term is sometimes used interchangeably with the term "Emotional Disturbance."

SEIT (Special Education Itinerant Teacher) - A licensed special education teacher who is assigned to a preschool child as part of their home-based program and who provides one-to-one specialized instruction.

SETSS (Special Education Teacher Support Services) - Part of the continuum of special education services that a CSE can offer to a classified student, or to a non-classified student who is "at risk" of educational failure. This specially designed and/or supplemental instruction, which used to be called "resource room," is provided by a special education teacher in a small group setting. The student can be taken out of their classroom to receive this service ("pull out"), or the service can be brought into the classroom ("push in"). It is usually provided for one or (at the most) two periods per day.

Self-Contained Class - A full-time small special education classroom for classified students.

Self-Stimulatory Behavior (also called **Stimming** or **Stereotypic Behaviors**) - Repetitive body movements or repetitive movement of objects. This behavior is common in children with developmental disabilities, particularly autism. Stereotypic behaviors can involve any one or all senses. Below are the five major senses and some examples of self-stimulatory behaviors involving them:

> **Visual** - staring at lights, repetitive blinking, moving fingers in front of the eyes, hand flapping, staring at spinning wheels

> **Auditory** - tapping ears, snapping fingers, making unintelligible vocal sounds, humming

> **Tactile** - rubbing the skin with one's hands or with another object, scratching

> **Vestibular** - rocking front to back, rocking side to side, spinning, head shaking

> **Taste/Gustatory** - placing body parts or objects in one's mouth, licking objects

Semantic Pragmatic Disorder - The communicative behavior of children who present with traits such as pathological talkativeness, deficient access to vocabulary and discourse comprehension, atypical choice of terms, and inappropriate conversational skills.

Sensorineural Hearing Loss - A type of hearing loss in which the root cause lies in the vestibulocochlear nerve, the inner ear, or central processing centers of the brain.

Sensory Gym - A therapeutic gym under the management and supervision of a certified occupational therapist that uses specifically designed equipment to provide sensory integration therapy to children with SID/Sensory Processing Disorder.

SID (Sensory Integration Dysfunction or Sensory Integration Disorder) - See **SPD (Sensory Processing Disorder)**

SLD (Specific Learning Disability) - A disorder in one or more of the basic psychological processes involved in understanding or in using language, spoken or written, which may manifest itself in the imperfect ability to listen, think, speak, read, write, spell, or do mathematical calculations, including conditions such as perceptual disabilities, brain injury, minimal brain dysfunction, dyslexia, and developmental aphasia. A specific learning disability does not include learning problems that are primarily the result of visual, hearing, or motor disabilities, of intellectual disabilities, of emotional disturbance, or of environmental, cultural, or economic disadvantages.

SLP (Speech - Language Pathologist) - Commonly referred to as a speech therapist, this master's-degree or doctorate-degree holding professional specializes in treating children with communication disorders as well as feeding and swallowing disorders. Speech is a separate function from language, and a speech pathologist can treat problems or dysfunctions in one or both areas. The main components of speech production are: phonation, which is the process of sound production; resonance; intonation, which is the variation of pitch; and voice, which includes aeromechanical components of respiration. The main components of language are: phonology, which is the manipulation of sound according to the rules of the language; morphology, which is the understanding and use of the minimal units of meaning; syntax, which is the grammar rules for constructing sentences in language; semantics, which is the interpretation of meaning from the signs or symbols of communication; and pragmatics, which is the social aspect of communication.

SNT (Special Needs Trust) - A specialized legal document designed to benefit an individual who has a disability. It can either be a "stand-alone" document or part of a Last Will and Testament. This type of Trust enables a person who has a physical or mental disability or an individual with a chronic or acquired illness to have, held in Trust for his or her benefit, an unlimited amount of assets. These assets are not considered countable assets for purposes of qualification for certain governmental benefits, such as SSI, Medicaid, subsidized housing, vocational rehabilitation, or other benefits based upon need. This type of Trust must be prepared by an attorney who has specific expertise in estate planning.

Social Promotion - The unofficial practice of promoting a student to the next grade, regardless of whether or when the child met necessary academic standards, in order to keep them with peers of their same age group. Although this is no longer permitted, it can still occur by the lowering of promotional standards on a student's IEP.

Social Skills Group - These are groups run by professionals where there is a focus on the acquisition and maintaining of appropriate social relationships. These programs are often used for children with nonverbal learning disabilities and high-functioning autism.

Spatial Relationships - The ability of an individual to relate self, objects, or parts of self to the environment in terms of size, position, distance, or direction.

SPD (Sensory Processing Disorder) - This is the newest term for, and is used synonymously with, SID (Sensory Integration Disorder or Sensory Integration Dysfunction). It is a neurological disorder resulting from the brain's inability to integrate certain information received from the body's basic sensory systems. These sensory systems are responsible for detecting sights, sounds, smells, tastes, temperatures, pain, and the position and movements of the body. The brain then forms a combined picture of this information in order for the body to make sense of its surroundings and react to them appropriately. The presence of a sensory processing disorder is typically detected in young children. While most children develop sensory integration during the course of ordinary childhood activities, which helps establish such things as the ability for motor planning and adapting to incoming sensations, other children's sensory integration abilities do not develop as efficiently. When their process is disordered, a variety of problems in learning, development or behavior become obvious. Those who have sensory processing disorder may be unable to respond to certain sensory information through planning and organizing what needs to be done in an appropriate and automatic manner.

The following are some signs of sensory processing disorder: oversensitivity to touch, movement, sights, or sounds; under-reactivity to touch, movement, sights, or sounds; tendency to be easily distracted; social and/or emotional problems; activity level that is unusually high or unusually low; physical clumsiness or apparent carelessness; impulsivity, the absence of self-control; difficulty in making transitions from one situation to another; inability to unwind or calm self; poor self-concept; decreased awareness of body, space, and boundaries; delays in speech, language, or motor skills; delays in academic achievement.

Special Education - Specially designed individualized or group instruction or special services or programs to meet the unique needs of students with disabilities. Special education services and programs are provided at no cost to the parent.

Speech and Language Impairment - One of the 13 classifications available under the IDEA. It means a communication disorder such as stuttering, impaired articulation, language impairment, or a voice impairment that adversely affects a child's educational performance.

SRO (State Review Officer) - An appointed official in Albany who serves as the first appeal officer to review the decision of an impartial hearing officer concerning the identification, evaluation, program, or placement of children who have, or are suspected of having, an educational disability.

SS (Scaled Score) - There are two types of test scores: raw scores and scaled scores. A raw score is a score without any sort of adjustment or transformation, such as the simple number of questions answered correctly. A scaled score is the results of some transformation applied to the raw score.

SSDI (Social Security Disability Insurance) - Cash benefits paid to individuals who are blind or have other disabilities and who have previously worked and paid into the Social Security System. There is no means test to qualify for this benefit.

SSI (Supplemental Security Income) - A supplemental cash benefits program administered by the Social Security Administration for individuals who are blind or have other disabilities, and who have little or no income or resources.

ST (Speech Therapy) - A related service provided by a licensed, certified speech pathologist to children who qualify under the IDEA or who are determined to be at risk. It is designed to address deficits in a student's auditory processing, articulation/phonological skills, comprehension and use of semantics, syntax, pragmatics, voice production, and fluency.

Stanford Binet - A standardized test that assesses IQ and cognitive abilities in children and adults ages 2 to 23. This test is designed to test intelligence in four areas including verbal reasoning, quantitative reasoning, abstract and visual reasoning, and short-term memory skills.

Stimming - See **Self-Stimulating Behavior**

Stipulation (or Stipulation of Settlement) - A document prepared when a parent and school district reach a settlement before the conclusion of an Impartial Hearing.

SubCSE (Subcommittees on Special Education) - In NYC, these are referred to as the School-Based Support Team (SBST).

Supplementary Aids and Services - A term used in the IDEA to describe the aids, services, and supports that are provided to children with disabilities who are being educated in regular education classes. Some examples of this can include assistive technology, or a one-on-one paraprofessional, a consultant teacher, or a behavior expert.

Tactile Defensiveness - A hypersensitivity to touch, which is usually indicative of a sensory processing disorder or some other developmental delay.

TAT (Thematic Apperception Test) - A projective psychological test that is widely used and researched. It is supposed to tap into a subject's unconscious to reveal repressed aspects of personality, motives, needs for achievement, power and intimacy, as well as problem-solving abilities.

TBI (Traumatic Brain Injury) - An acquired injury to the brain caused by an external physical force, resulting in total or partial functional disability, or psychosocial impairment, or both, which adversely affects a child's educational performance. The term applies to open or closed head injuries resulting in impairments in one or more areas such as cognition, language, memory, attention, reasoning, abstract thinking, judgment, problem solving, sensory, perceptual, motor abilities, psychosocial behavior, physical functions, information processing, and speech. The term does not apply to brain injuries that are congenital or degenerative, or to brain injuries induced by birth trauma.

TEACCH (The Education of Autistic and Communicatively Challenged Children) - A methodology which uses an approach called structured teaching, which emphasizes a highly structured and predictable classroom environment using visual learning. It is often used to teach children with autism and other communication disabilities. *www.teacch.com*

Therapeutic Day Program - An instructional placement for students with serious emotional disturbance in which aspects of treatment for the emotional difficulty are incorporated into the school program. As the name implies, this is not a residential program but rather a program where a student receives therapy at the school during the school day and continues to reside at home.

Therapeutic Residential School - Sometimes referred to as a therapeutic boarding school. This is a school where children reside as well as attend school. This type of program is for children with serious emotional disturbances who cannot function in a day program and require a 24-hour therapeutic setting in order to receive any type of education.

Three-Prong Burlington/Carter Test - This three-prong test was first established in the 1985 Burlington case, and then expanded in the 1993 Carter case. It establishes three prongs that have to be satisfied in order for a parent to be awarded tuition reimbursement at an Impartial Hearing or appeal. These are: (1) the placement proposed by the school did not comply with the IDEA's requirement of a free and appropriate public education (FAPE); (2) the parent's private placement is appropriate, meaning it is reasonably calculated to confer an educational benefit to the child; and (3) "equitable considerations" justify an award. (See Chapter Five for a detailed explanation.)

Title 1 - A federal funding program for schools, specifically designed to help students who are behind academically or "at risk" of falling behind. Funding is based on the number of low-income children in that school, generally those eligible for free lunch. Schools who receive Title 1 funding are required to involve parents in deciding how these funds are to be spent.

Tourette Syndrome - A condition with onset in childhood characterized by compulsive arm movements, facial tics, grunting, groaning, and shouting. Aside from coprolalia (the excessive and uncontrollable use of foul or obscene language), there is often echolalia (the involuntary parrot-like repetition or echoing of a word or sentence just spoken by another person). Children with Tourette syndrome do not usually curse out of anger or displeasure, but rather out of uncontrollable compulsion.

Transition Plan - There are two types of transition plans, one when a child transitions from early intervention into CPSE, and the other when a student is in high school and beginning to think about post-high school programs/services/opportunities. A transition plan is the section of the IEP that outlines goals and services for the student based on individual needs, skills, and interests. Transition planning is used to identify and develop goals that need to be accomplished during the current school year to assist the student in meeting their post-high school goals.

Transitional Support Services - Temporary services provided to a teacher in order to aid in providing appropriate services to a student as the student moves to a less restrictive environment. These services must be identified on the child's IEP.

Trienneal - An evaluation that is conducted by a school district every three years.

TTD/TTY - A Tele-typewriting device used by the deaf or hard of hearing in lieu of a telephone.

Turning Five Review Meeting - Occurs sometime in the spring of the calendar year in which a child turns five years old. At this CSE meeting, eligibility for special education services must be determined, a specific classification identified, an IEP developed, and a placement recommended.

*Type 1 - A form used by the NYC DOE, which is completed at an annual review that indicates that there is no change to the child's IEP.

*Type 2 - A form used by the NYC DOE, which is completed at an annual review when there is a change to the child's IEP.

*Type 3 - A form used by the NYC DOE, when a member of the IEP team (often the child's teacher) or another member of the school staff (such as a related service provider) believes that a child requires an increase or decrease in services or a change of program. It is a request by school personnel for a SBST/CSE review of the IEP, and it requires the involvement of the school psychologist.

Unilateral Placement - A placement made by a parent without the recommendation, approval, or consent of the CSE, but for which the parent looks to the school district for tuition. While this term is most often used when referring to a child's placement in a private special education school, it can also be used for a private therapist or other services for which a parent initiates and pays for on his or her own. A parent can sue for tuition reimbursement for a unilateral placement if a child has or should have an IEP.

Variance - A mechanism used in order to waive a specific regulation or rule. A "child-specific variance" is used by a NYS-approved private special education school or a public school when a classroom exceeds the number of students it is suppose to have. A "school variance" is when a principal grants permission for a student who does not live within the catchment area to attend that school. Both types of variances are infrequently given, but can still be obtained if a sibling attends a school, or if a parent works within that catchment area. There is no requirement that a principal grant such permission; it is completely discretionary.

VESID (New York State Office of Vocational and Educational Services for Individuals with Disabilities) - An office within the NYS Education Department, providing services to eligible individuals to prepare them for suitable jobs. It also helps people with disabilities that are having difficulty keeping their jobs. To be eligible for VESID services, an individual must have a physical, mental, emotional, or learning disability that interferes with their ability to work. There must also be a reasonable chance that the individual will become gainfully employed if he/she receives rehabilitation services. Eligibility for services is determined by a review of the individual's medical records and, in some cases, by the submission of new medical and vocational evaluations. *www.vesid.nysed.gov*

Vestibular - The sense of movement; input from the inner ear about equilibrium, gravitational changes, movement experiences, and position in space. When a child has difficulty with his or her vestibular system, it can be a symptom of sensory processing disorder.

VIQ (Verbal IQ) - A measure of acquired knowledge, verbal reasoning and comprehension, the application of verbal skills and information to the solution of new problems, the ability to process verbal information and the ability to think with words. The VIQ provides information about language processing, reasoning, attention, and verbal learning and memory.

Visual - The input relating to sight; a child's ability to correctly perceive, discriminate, process and respond to what one sees. When a child exhibits difficulty with this, it can be a symptom of a sensory processing disorder.

Visual Discrimination - The ability to discern likenesses and differences in colors, shapes, objects, words, and symbols.

Visual Impairment - One of the 13 classifications available in New York State—including blindness or impairment in vision that, even with correction, adversely affects a child's educational performance. The term includes both partial sight and blindness.

Visual Motor - An ability to coordinate the eyes with the movement of the hands, frequently referred to as hand-eye coordination.

Visuospatial - Of or relating to visual perception or spatial relationships among objects.

WAIS (Wechsler Adult Intelligent Scale) - An intelligence test that generates an IQ for subjects 16 years of age and older.

Whole Language - A literacy philosophy and method of instruction that places emphasis on meaning and strategy for learning. Whole language is not a systemized approach, but rather a philosophy that assumes that reading and general language competencies are acquired through integrated use instead of through learning separate, finite skills, such as word attack, comprehension, and vocabulary. It relies heavily on the use of literature and trade books.

WIAT (Wechsler Individual Achievement Test) - A measure or test of academic achievement skills for both children, ages four and above, as well as adults. There are four basic scales: Reading, Math, Written

Language, and Oral Language. Within these scales there are a combined total of nine subtest scores.

Wilson Reading System - A research-based reading and writing program, which is the flagship program of Wilson Language Training. This program is based on Orton-Gillingham principles and is a highly structured remedial program that directly teaches the structure of the language to even the most challenged readers, i.e., students (grade 2 and beyond) and adults who have been unable to learn with other teaching strategies or who may require multisensory language instruction.

WPPSI (Wechsler Preschool and Primary Scale of Intelligence) - An intelligence test for young children ages 3 years old to 7 years and 3 months old.

WISC (Wechsler Intelligence Test for Children) - An intelligence test which generates an IQ for children between the ages of 6 and 16. It is comprised of ten core subtests and five supplemental ones. These subtests then generate a Full Scale score (FSIQ), as well as four composite scores known as "indexes". These are: Verbal Comprehension (VCI), Perceptual Reasoning (PRI), Processing Speed (PSI) and Working Memory (WMI).

WJ III (Woodcock Johnson, Third Edition) - An academic achievement test commonly used by school districts.

YAI (Young Adult Institute) - A nonprofit health and human services organization serving people with developmental and learning disabilities and their families throughout New York State. *www.yai.org*

THANK YOU

I started my career in 1973 as a social worker. In my clinical role, I worked with children with special needs, teenagers, and their parents. For 36 years I was also one of the owners and directors of Summit Camp, the largest summer camp for children with special needs. It was at Summit that I learned about "our kids," their challenges, their abilities, and their profound sensitivities and talents. In 1988, I entered law school for the sole purpose of becoming an advocate and champion for our kids. My first job as a lawyer was given to me by my mentor, camp partner, and friend, Mayer Stiskin.

I am forever indebted to Mayer, who taught me not only about children with special needs, but also about the ethics of business, and how important it is to treat each person the way in which you would want to be treated. It was Mayer who encouraged me to go to law school and pursue a career as a special education attorney.

Since graduating in 1991, I have worked as an attorney practicing in the field of special education law. But before I was even admitted to the bar, I worked as a pro bono advocate at the renowned agency, Advocates for Children. It was at Advocates for Children that I met Joan Harrington.

Joan is one of New York City's premier advocates, and she continues to enjoy a wonderful reputation in the special education community. She took me under her wing, and sat right alongside me at the first Impartial Hearing I ever did. And like a mother bird that knows when to toss her chick out of the nest, she sent me off flying.

There are some people in life that you never forget. Thank you, Mayer and Joan, for the lasting impact you have had on my career.

But of all the teachers and mentors in my career, it is you—the thousands of devoted and selfless parents—who have taught me the most. For those of you who have met with me, you know that next to my own children and family, my work is my greatest passion. This passion is continuously re-ignited whenever I meet with parents and become a partner in their child's educational journey.

I would be remiss if I did not also thank my devoted staff who read, re-read, edited, and re-edited this book—and who also had to listen to me talk about it for the last ten years. Without their professionalism, devotion, respect, and love I could not have done this. They are: Jesse Cutler, Lara Damashek, Jaime Chlupsa, Ben Foley, Susan Foley, Greg Cangiano, Diana Gersten, Linda Goldman, Tevi Graham, Teri Horowitz, Sonia Mendez-Castro, Will Meyer, Sheila Pollak, Marcie Rodriguez, Abbie Smith, Cynthia Vientos, Victoria Wagnerman, and Brett Weinstein.

Thank you also to Wendy Borges for her gorgeous illustrations and hard work designing this book, to Lu Borges for his assistance, and also to Eliyanna Kaiser for her feedback and proofreading.

And most of all, thank you to my own parents, children, and husband—Ruth and Irving Pagirsky, Josh and Elana Skyer, and Jonathan Goldberg—who have been, and will always be, my role models, inspiration, and my greatest champions. The gift of family is eternal...

REGINA SKYER is a leading special education lawyer known throughout New York State. After enjoying a fifteen-year career as a social worker and special education administrator, she entered the City University of New York Public Interest Law School in 1988 for the sole purpose of embarking on a legal career representing special needs children and their families. Balancing her jobs of mother, summer camp director, social worker, and student, Regina was recognized as a leading student in her graduating class of 1991, and was admitted to the New York Bar in 1992.

Before opening her own practice, Law Offices of Regina Skyer & Associates, Regina worked as a pro bono volunteer attorney at Advocates for Children, and then for a short time at the NYC Board of Education Office of Legal Services.

Regina's involvement in every aspect of her firm's day-to-day operation is obvious. She meets with new clients and helps parents find meaningful educational programs and opportunities for their children, always working closely with educational consultants, neuropsychologists, evaluators, and other professionals.

Regina brings a unique mix of social work, special education experience, and legal background to her work, and she is passionate about helping empower parents to advocate for their children. She not only knows the law, but also shares her extensive knowledge of existing schools, programs, and services in order to effectively guide parents in what can otherwise be an overwhelming process. In her first consultation with a family, she presents them with options, explains the legal process, and helps plan an initial strategy for their child's education.

Regina is a much sought-after lecturer on special needs education and conducts parent seminars throughout New York State. Throughout her professional career, Regina has served on the board of private schools and charitable organizations, and she currently volunteers teaching school children through the NYC Museum of Jewish Heritage.

How to Survive Turning 5 is part of Regina's long-awaited six-book "How to Survive" series, which includes in its forthcoming offerings an updated edition of her co-authored 1986 book, *What Do You Do After High School?*.

To learn about her upcoming appearances, and to stay up to date on special education policy and law, please visit her indispensible blog at www.skyerlaw.com/blog.